ROYAL COURT THEATRE and

ROGER BERLIND GLADYS NEDERLANDER FREDERICK ZOLLO

in association with THOM MOUNT *and* BONNIE TIMMERMANN

present the

ROYAL COURT THEATRE PRODUCTION

DEATH AND THE MAIDEN

by ARIEL DORFMAN

PENNY DOWNIE

HUGH ROSS

DANNY WEBB

Associate Producers 126 SECOND AVE. CORP. *and* RONALD J. KASTNER

directed by LINDSAY POSNER

associate director BRIAN STIRNER

designed by IAN MacNEIL

lighting designed by KEVIN SLEEP

First performance at the Duke of York's Theatre: 11 February 1992

First performance with this cast: 10 August 1992

DUKE OF YORK'S THEATRE

Sole Proprietor: Duke of York's Theatre Ltd

St Martin's Lane, London WC2N 4BG

Box Office 071-836 5122

SERIOUS SUCCESS

*In this age of built-in
obsolescence, it seems odd that
the one new product it
appears no-one wants to buy
is a play. Over the past
couple of years, celebrated
critics have lamented the
demise of The Big New Play
while the Arts Council have
wrung their hands over
statistics showing that new
plays now make up less than
7% of the national repertoire.
Theatres are blamed for lack
of nerve. Audiences are
blamed for lack of interest.
Critics are blamed for lack of
taste. Everyone wants a classic
or the stage adaptation of a
favourite novel. However,
unfashionable though it may
be, one could argue that the
bell-ringers are tolling the
death knell too soon.*

*From it inception in 1956,
the Royal Court has been
dedicated to the production of
new plays by contemporary
playwrights and, from the
beginning, has enjoyed both
success and notoriety. The
first major hit was Look Back
In Anger by John Osborne.
Initially, slated by most of the
critics, the play found favour*

BENT PHOTO JOHN HAYNES

*with Kenneth Tynan and a
whole new generation of
theatre-goers. Between 1956
and 1968 it was revived four
times, before moving to the
West End. It is now regarded
as a modern classic. From
that moment on, the English
Stage Company did not look
back. Other notable West End
transfers have included:
Osborne's The Entertainer
with Laurence Olivier (1957)
and Inadmissable Evidence
(1964); Arnold Wesker's
Roots (1959); Christopher
Hampton's When Did You
Last See My Mother? which,
when it moved to the Comedy
Theatre in 1966, made
Hampton, at 20, the youngest
playwright in living memory
to have a play presented in
the West End; Teeth and
Smiles by David Hare
(1975); Mary O'Malley's
Once a Catholic (1977);*

*Bent by Martin Sherman
(1979) and The Normal
Heart by Larry Kramer
(1986). In recent years,
West End transfers have
included Caryl Churchill's
timely and acerbic money
market comedy Serious Money
(1987); George C Wolfe's
American black musical
The Colored Museum (1987)
and Timberlake Wertenbaker's
moving portrayal story of
convict life in Australian
settlements in Our Country's
Good (1989).*

OUR COUNTRY'S GOOD
PHOTO JOHN HAYNES

Much of the work generated by the Royal Court, like Death and the Maiden, starts life in the experimental studio, the Theatre Upstairs. In 1973, the Rocky Horror Picture Show was produced in this studio space. It seized the public imagination, transferred to two Chelsea cinemas and then moved to the Comedy Theatre where it ended its run, 7 years after opening at the Court. In 1982, Andrea Dunbar, at the age of 16, won the Young Writers' Festival. Her play The Arbor was produced. It was so successful Upstairs, that she extended the play which was then produced Downstairs. This new version was subsequently made into the film Rita, Sue and Bob Too. In 1986, Jim Cartwright's Road moved from Upstairs to the Main house

and was then re-mounted at the Lincoln Centre, New York. It has since been performed all over the world.

The hunger for new work remains. A theatrical success may often be picked up by the sister media, film and television. Throughout the Royal Court's history, plays have been turned into films and have been seen nationally and internationally. Such films include: Look Back in Anger and The Entertainer; Ann Jellicoe's The Knack (1961); Wallace Shawn's My Dinner with André (1981); Terry Johnson's Insignificance (1982), Paul Kimber's Not Quite Jerusalem (1982); Manfred Karge's Man to Man (1988) and The Conquest of the South Pole (1988) and of course, The Rocky Horror Picture Show. Television films include: Ron Hutchinson's

Rat in the Skull (1984); Road (1986), Iain Heggie's Wholly Healthy Glasgow (1989) and Caryl Churchill's Top Girls (1982, revived and broadcast 1991).

So it seems that the age of the new play is not yet over. Contemporary plays continue to offer a fresh perspective on our world and a way of asking vital questions. Death and The Maiden is a case in point.

Mel Kenyon
Literary Manager
January 1992

ROAD PHOTO JOHN HAYNES

RAT IN THE SKULL PHOTO JOHN HAYNES
right MAN TO MAN PHOTO JOHN HAYNES

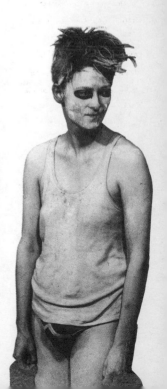

DEATH AND THE MAIDEN

by ARIEL DORFMAN

Cast in order of appearance

Paulina Salas
PENNY DOWNIE

Gerardo Escobar
DANNY WEBB

Roberto Miranda
HUGH ROSS

Director LINDSAY POSNER
Associate Director BRIAN STIRNER
Designer IAN MacNEIL
Lighting KEVIN SLEEP
Sound BRYAN BOWEN
Company Stage Manager SHEENA LINDEN
Deputy Stage Manager MICHELLE ENRIGHT
Assistant Stage Manager PETER WAKEMAN
Sound Operator RICHARD PUGH
Assistant Director STEVEN DOBBIN
Wardrobe Mistress CATHRYN JOHNS
Wardrobe Assistant MARCELLA MARTINELLI
Set built by STAGE PRODUCTION SERVICES
Set painted by PADDY HAMILTON
Cyclorama painted by MARTIN JEZIERSKI
Leaflet, poster, programme design SIGHTLINES
Production photographs MARK DOUET

The Royal Court Theatre would like to thank the following for their help with this production: Clarins (UK) Ltd, Johnger Ltd, Belling Ltd, Royal National Theatre Studio, LIFT, Vicente Alegria of Chile Demecratico, Maria Berho and Florenticia Varas of the Chilean Embassy, Gaston Hidalgo, Francisco Morates and the Medical Foundation for the Care of Victims of Torture, Nidia Castro and Roberto Sarah, Amnesty International, hair by Carole of Edmunds, Beauchamp Place.

The time is the present. The place a country that is probably Chile, but could be any other country that has given itself a democratic government after a long period of dictatorship.

There is no interval.

ARIEL DORFMAN

Author and playwright. Born in Argentina in 1942 and forced into exile from Chile in 1973. His numerous books have been translated into over 20 languages.

Other plays include: Widows and Reader. Novels include: Hard Rain, Mascara, The Last Song of Manuel Sendero and Widows. Non-fictional work: How to Read Donald Duck (with Armand Mattelart); The Empire's Old Clothes, and Some Write to the Future.

PENNY DOWNIE

For the Royal Court: Berlin Bertie.

Other theatre includes: Scenes from a Marriage (Wyndham's Theatre); The Plantagenets, Art of Success, Macbeth, A Winter's Tale, Crimes in Hot Countries, The Castle, Dream Play, Today, Richard III, Romeo and Juliet, A Midsummer Night's Dream (RSC); A Map of the World, P.S. Your Cat is Dead (Sydney Theatre Company); Privates on Parade (Perth Playhouse); Ten Times Table (Marian Street Theatre); The Shrew, The Matchmaker, Shoemakers'

Holiday, The Miser, Streetcar Named Desire (Old Tote Theatre); Fiddler on the Roof, The Man, Savages, See How They Run (Tasmanian Theatre Company; East Lynne, Music Hall (Downstage Theatre Wellington).

Television includes: Inspector Morse; Underbelly; Ex; Stanley and the Woman; A Taste for Death; Campaign; Minder; The Sullivans; Prisoner Cell Block H.

Films include: Lionheart, Wetherby, Cross Talk, Around the Bend.

HUGH ROSS

For the Royal Court: Falkland Sound, Victory (with Joint Stock).

Other theatre includes: Hedda Gabler (Abbey Theatre Dublin; Playhouse, London); As You Like It, All's Well That Ends Well (RSC); Bussy D'Ambois (Old Vic); Mary Stuart (Greenwich); The Cid, Twelfth Night (Cheek By Jowl); The Cruscible (Young Vic); The Prime of Miss Jean Brodie (Royal Exchange).

Television includes: An Ungentlemanly Act; Poirot; The Advocates; Misterioso, Kinsey;

She's Been Away; Taggart; The Pickwick Papers; Anna Karenina; Falkland Sound.

Radio includes: Dreams and Censorship; The View for Westminster Bridge; Observe the Sons of Ulster Marching Towards the Somme; Felix Randal; The Cherry Orchard; The Potting Shed; Talk of Love and War.

Films include: Nightbreed; Patriot Games.

BRIAN STIRNER

Theatre includes: Across the Ferry, Boys Mean Business, Millfire, The Touch, Marshalling Yard, Fatherland (Bush Theatre); The Attractions, Leaving Home, Under the Web, Holy Days, Munich Athens (Soho Poly); Everything in the Garden (Palace Theatre Watford); Educating Rita, Treats (Mill at Sonning). Past Director at Soho Poly and Artistic Director of the Bush Theatre.

DANNY WEBB

For the Royal Court: Serious Money (at Wyndham's and in New York), Carnival Wars.

Other theatre includes: Back Up

the Hearse (Hampstead Theatre); The Pool of Bethesda (Richmond Theatre); Hamlet (Orange Tree); Night Must Fall (Greenwich Theatre); The Nest, Californian Dog Fight (Bush Theatre); Progress (Lyric Hammersmith); The Gardens of England, As I Lay Dying, Murderers, Mandragola (Royal National Theatre); Up for None (National Workshop); The Rocky Horror Show (Nottingham Playhouse); American Days (Bristol Old Vic); Privates on Parade (Northcott Exeter); What the Butler Saw (Palace Theatre Watford); I'm Talking About Jerusalem (Shaw Theatre).

Television includes: Head Hunters; Young Indy; Clubland; The Jazz Detective; Made in Heaven; Confusions of a Modern Man; The Saint; Boon; Poirot; Hard Cases; Tales of Sherwood Forest; Bergerac; Intimate Contact; Slip-Up; Do You Know the Milky Way; More Lives Than One; Tucker's Luck; Video Stars; Brookside; Whatever Happened to the Hero; Star Struck; The Other Arf; Passamore; We'll Meet Again; MacKenzie; The Imitation Game; The Racing Game; Jackanory Playhouse; Twelfth Night.

Films include: Aliens 3; Robin Hood; Henry V; Didn't You Kill My Brother; Defence of the Realm; Billy the Kid and the Green Vampire; The Year of the Quiet Sun; The Unapproachable; No Exit.

Records: No John No (with Forward Fifties).

LINDSAY POSNER

For the Royal Court: Sleeping Ugly (Young Writer's Festival 1991); No one Sees the Video; True Love Stories; The Little Rabbi; Blood; American Bagpipes (also Glasgow Mayfest); Downfall; Ambulance; Built on Sand; Ficky Stingers (Young Writers' Festival 1986). Other theatre includes: Much Ado About Nothing (Regent's Park); Leonce and Lena (Sheffield Crucible); The Doctor of Honour (Cheek by Jowl Tour); The Stillborn (Soho Poly).

KEVIN SLEEP

Lighting Designer

For the Royal Court: Downfall and Sore Throats. West End credits include: The House of Bernarda Alba; The Foreigners; Fascinating Aida; Up on the Roof; Eartha Kitt in Concert; Prin; Blues in the Night; Woman in Black and Other People's Money. Other work includes: The Old Devils (Theatr Clwyd); Painting Churches (Nuffield Southampton and Playhouse); The Real Don Juan (Oxford Stage Company); The Winter's Tale (Royal Exchange); Jock Tamsons Bairns and Carmen (Communicado Theatre Company); Much Ado About Nothing (Regent's Park); Blitz! (Northern Stage Company); and regular designs for Lyric Hammersmith, Royal Lyceum, Edinburgh, The Sheffield Crucible and Churchill Theatre, Bromley. Opera designs include: Greek and 63 Dream Palace (Munich; Rigoletto (WNO tour); Wexford Opera Festival; Eugene Onegin (Scottish Opera Go Round); and revival of Greek (ENO).

ORIGINAL CAST
Juliet Stevenson (top)
Bill Paterson and Michael Byrne

DEATH AND THE MAIDEN –

a brief performance history

Death and the Maiden was first seen in this country as a rehearsed reading at the ICA, in November 1990, presented by the Censored Plays Project.

It was first performed in the Theatre Upstairs on 4 July 1991, presented by the London International Festival of Theatre and the Royal Court, in association with the Royal National Theatre Studio, as part of the Cross References season featured in LIFT '91. It moved to the Royal Court Main Stage on 31 October 1991, and transferred to the Duke of York's Theatre on 11 February 1992. The first performance with the present cast was on 10 August 1992.

The progress of Death and the Maiden illustrates how theatres in this country help each other for the benefit of playwrights and audiences alike. Without the Censored Plays Project a tiny, un-funded group, the play may never have come to light in Britain. The London International Festival of Theatre was one of the initiators of the Cross References season of international plays' and contributed to the production costs. The Royal National Theatre Studio helped significantly with the costs of rehearsal.

The Royal Court, "Britain's National Theatre of New Writing" provided the opportunity for the play to be produced and presented to its best advantage. Our grateful thanks to all these contributors. Other productions of Death and The Maiden are planned around the world. A new production opened on Broadway on 18 February 1992 and there will be a Hollywood film directed by Roman Polanski.

SECOND CAST
Geraldine James

FOR ROYAL COURT THEATRE

Artistic Director MAX STAFFORD-CLARK

Artistic Director Designate STEPHEN DALDRY

General Manager GRAHAM COWLEY

Financial Administrator MARK RUBINSTEIN

Production Manager BO BARTON

Chief Electrician JOHANNA TOWN

Master Carpenter GUY VIGGERS

Wardrobe Supervisor JENNIFER COOK

Casting Director LISA MAKIN

Marketing Manager GUY CHAPMAN

Sales Manager DAVID BROWNLEE

FOR ROYAL COURT THEATRE
PRODUCTIONS LTD
Directors:
JOHN MORTIMER *(Chairman)*
STUART BURGE CBE
ANTHONY C BURTON
GRAHAM COWLEY
HARRIET CRUICKSHANK
ROBERT FOX
DEREK GRANGER
SONIA MELCHETT
ALAN RICKMAN
MAX STAFFORD-CLARK

Press JOY SAPIEKA ASSOCIATES
(071-383 5877)
Costume Supervisor IONA KENRICK

The English Stage Company at the Royal Court Theatre receives financial support from:

The Arts Council of Great Britain
(and an Incentive Funding Award),
The London Boroughs Grants Committee,
The Royal Borough of Kensington and Chelsea.

Its principal sponsors are:
Barclays Bank plc,
British Gas North Thames,
John Cass's Foundation,
CitiBank, Marks & Spencer,
The Rayne Foundation and
Wilde Sapte, Solicitors.

The English Stage Company is
a registered charity number 231242

DORFMAN
AND
DEATH AND
THE MAIDEN

Matthew d'Ancona

When I interviewed Ariel Dorfman last July at the Royal Court, he was still making fine adjustments to the text of Death and the Maiden, a play which, he reminded me, he had written in a matter of weeks. A few last minute changes were necessary, he said, before he returned to Los Angeles to work on another project and plan his teaching programmme at Duke University in North Carolina. The writer was full of enthusiasm for Lindsay Posner's production, the first to be staged outside Chile, but not even he could have predicted the extent of its success in the months that followed and the critical acclaim which has smoothed its passage to the West End.

What is the source of this play's power and the spell which it casts upon audiences night after night? One answer, I suspect, is that Death and the Maiden tackles some of the most important political questions of our time, but does so in a chamber setting, deftly grafting the personal onto the political. Dorfman himself, born in Argentina but a Chilean citizen, was forced into exile after Pinochet's 1973 military coup, returning home in 1990 to discover a country anxious to forget its recent history. He is no stranger to the personal cost of turbulent political change.

Death and the Maiden is the story of a woman's agonised past, her desire to bring that past to light and her bid for justice in the face of a society which offers only compromise. The play may have a Latin American feel to it, but its moral terrain is universal. More than anything, it is an exploration of censorship and

the plight of the marginalised. Paulina's predicament is that of all individuals and peoples whose voices are suppressed, what Dorfman calls 'The censored zones of humanity'. In his imaginative world, story-telling is a form of liberation and silence a form of repression. "People in misdeveloped, twisted lands may not be able to dominate what really happens to them," he has written, "but they can at least control the stories they tell".

In this sense, Death and the Maiden is a play of its time. In the last few years, glasnost has become a keyword in the vocabulary of political change, as democratic movements around the world have acknowledged that the right to free expression underpins other basic human and civil rights.

From Zambia to Nepal, a new democratic esperanto has taken root and dislodged regimes that have previously seemed immovable. The revolutions in eastern Europe of 1989 were fought in samizdat under banners bearing the Hussite motto, Truth shall prevail (Pravda Vitezi), as half a continent threw off the yoke of censorship and discovered the possibilities (and pitfalls) of political freedom. Havel, the dissident writer turned president, personified the importance of the unchained word to this historic moment — just as Dorfman has become an inspirational figure in Chile where his poems are reproduced on political posters.

Death and the Maiden speaks this fresh political language with a passion and a sense of history that transcend mere topicality. It probably says as much about the new democracies as The Crucible said about McCarthyism. But part of its strength as an exercise in political theatre is its complexity. Dorfman understands that freedom is brittle, fraught with danger and contradiction, and his play is a

debate rather than a polemic. He permits each of his characters — victim, alleged torturer and mediator — moments of legitimacy, and beckons the audience out of the glare of political certainty and into the shadows of ambiguity.

His play asks how fledgling democracies should treat their toppled dictators and how those whose lives have been shattered can co-exist with their former oppressors. Inspired by the Chilean commission appointed in April 1990 to investigate the human rights violations of the Pinochet years, Dorfman wondered what would happen if a husband and wife found themselves answering these questions in different ways.

In Gerardo, the lawyer who must sift through the ugly debris of a fallen dictatorship, he has created a symbol of ambitious pragmatism, a man who wants to see justice done but also hopes to keep his own boat and that of his homeland on an even keel. "We're going to suffocate from so much equanimity", says Paulina to her husband as he urges her once again to be rational and reconsider her actions. What, she asks, is the value of a system of justice which conspires to suppress the truth?

To survive and prosper, democracies need writing like this, bold in scope, rich in nuance and unafraid of troubling paradoxes. Writers, Dorfman told me, should not shy away from grand ideals and aspirations in their work. "There's a place for great themes and great ambitions", he said. "Art is one of the few spaces still left where we can deal with enormously important issues. We've got to be very pragmatic and we've got to dream a lot". This, I think, is the message of hope at the heart of his dark and extraordinary play.

Matthew d'Ancona works for The Times and is a fellow of All Souls College, Oxford.

FROM THE ROYAL COURT THEATRE

'dazzling social comedy'

WHAT'S ON

stockard channing

john guare's

SIX

degrees of separation

'a triumph'

INDEPENDENT ON SUNDAY

booking until 31 october

comedy theatre

071 867 1045 cc 867 1111

TICKET MASTER

071 379 4444

THE OLIVIER BUILDING APPEAL

The Royal Court Theatre was very proud of Lord Olivier's patronage of our Appeal. It continues in his name as a memorial to his life and talent and we are honoured that Joan Plowright, the Lady Olivier, is now our new Patron.

The Appeal, launched in June 1988 (The Royal Court's 100th Anniversary Year) had a target of £800,000 to repair and refurbish the fabric of the theatre building.

Visitors to the Royal Court are now beginning to benefit from the results of 'our continuing appeal' and we hope that you will enjoy the ambience and facilities of the Stalls and Circle Bars. The extensive refurbishment and renovation of these areas has been made possible through the generosity of donors to the Olivier Building Appeal.

We have nearly reached our 1988 'half-way target'. There is still so much work to be done — especially if you ever have the opportunity to look backstage and in the offices!

If you would like to help, and indeed would like 'a guided tour' to convince you of our needs, please telephone Nicki Shindler on 071 730 5174.

'Secure the Theatre's future, and take it forwards towards the new century. For the health of the whole theatrical life of Britain it is essential that this greatly all-providing theatre we love so much and wish so well continues to prosper'.

Laurence Olivier (1988)

(Covenant forms are available should you wish to make a regular donation)

I would like to donate to The Olivier Building Appeal
(Registered Charity Number 231242)

I ENCLOSE A CHEQUE MADE PAYABLE TO
THE OLIVIER BUILDING APPEAL
OR
PLEASE DEBIT MY ARTSCARD/ACCESS/VISA/AMEX ACCOUNT

☐☐☐☐☐☐☐☐☐☐☐☐☐☐☐☐

£

SIGNATURE

EXPIRY DATE

NAME

ADDRESS

POSTCODE

TELEPHONE DAY

EVENING

Return to The Olivier Building Appeal, Royal Court Theatre, Sloane Square, London, SW1W 8AS

THE NATIONAL ART COLLECTIONS FUND

is Britain's premier art charity

Last year we gave over £2 million to our museums and galleries to help buy works of fine and decorative art. This *Portrait of Anna Aagaard* by Gabriele Münter was acquired by Leicestershire Museum and Art Gallery with the help of a purchase grant from the National Art Collections Fund. •

We rely entirely on members' subscriptions, gifts and bequests; we receive no government funding. Members enjoy benefits including The Art Quarterly of the National Art Collections Fund, filled with articles by distinguished writers covering a broad spectrum of the visual arts; a programme of special events nationwide; free entry to art musems; and concessionary rates to many major exhibitions.

Annual membership costs £15; for more details of the benefits of membership, call 071–821 0404 or write to us at 20 John Islip Street, London SW1P 4JX.

Serious Money

(Wyndham's Theatre, 1987-8)

Our Country's Good

(Garrick Theatre, 1989-90)

Death and the Maiden

(Duke of York's Theatre, 1992)

All of these plays started life at the Royal Court Theatre. The Royal Court is the cradle of the best new plays in England.

You could have caught these hit plays and many more like them, at a fraction of the cost of the West End, and had priority booking for their very first performance.

The secret is to be a Member of the Royal Court Theatre Society.

These are the benefits:

• **Special priority booking** *for both Members' performances and the rest of the advertised run, a week before tickets go on general sale.*

• *Top price tickets in the main house* **reduced to £4** *for previews and selected other performances.*

Each member may buy two reduced rate tickets per production.

• *Tickets for the Theatre Upstairs (normally £5-£8)* **reduced to £4** *for previews and selected other performances.•*

Each member may buy **two** *reduced rate tickets per production.*

• *Regular Member's newsletter giving you advance information about the productions and special ticket offers for other theatres.*

• *Inclusion on the Royal Court's mailing list.*

All this for only £12 per year.

There are other patronage schemes for those who would like to be more closely associated with "Britain's national theatre of new writing"

Friends *For £40 (£60 for a joint subscription) you will be entitled to one (or two) complimentary tickets for each production. You will receive all other benefits of the Members.*

Associates *For £400 you will be entitled to four complimentary top price tickets for all Main House productions, and two tickets to all plays in the Theatre Upstairs.*
You will receive all the benefits of the Members and appear in the programme of the Main House productions.

Patrons *For £1000 you can make a personal appearance in our programmes, receive an invitation to the special event of the year and be entitled to six complimentary top price tickets for each production. You will receive all the benefits of the Members.*

Corporate Patrons *There is in addition the facility to entertain clients at the productions, and by arrangement at receptions after the show with members of the cast.*

For further information contact the Box Office (071 730 5174).

Patrons
Gerald Anholt
Diana Bliss
Michael Hoffman
Celia Imrie
Timberlake Wertenbaker
Irene Worth

Corporate Patrons
AdvanPress
Alan Baxter and Associates
Burlington Investments Ltd
Carlton Communications
Expedier plc
Peters Fraser & Dunlop Artists
Forsyte Kerman, Solicitors
Penguin Books Ltd

The Sunday Times
Thames Television
Michael Winner Ltd

Associates
Barclays Bank plc
David Capelli
Michael Codron
Jeremy Conway
Allan Davis
Mrs Henny Gestetner
Trevor Ingman
London Arts Discovery Tours
Patricia Marmont
Nick Hern Books
Greville Poke
Richard Wilson

DUKE OF YORK'S THEATRE LTD

The Producers of DEATH AND THE MAIDEN wish to acknowledge financial support received from the Theatre Investment Fund, a registered charity, which invests money in many commercial productions, runs seminars for new producers and raises money for the commercial theatre.

If you love the theatre and wish to promote its future, please consider making a gift to the Fund.

For further information regarding the Fund and its activities, please contact: Chief Executive, Theatre Investment Fund Limited, 18-20 Maiden Lane, London WC2E 7NH. Telephone 071 836 9245.

DEATH AND THE MAIDEN
A Play in Three Acts by

ARIEL DORFMAN

Translated from the Spanish original,
LA MUERTE Y LA DONCELLA
by ARIEL DORFMAN

**This play is for Harold Pinter
and María Elena Duvauchelle**

ARIEL DORFMAN

Ariel Dorfman, born in Argentina in 1942, is a Chilean citizen who was forced into exile after the 1973 coup that overthrew Salvador Allende. His numerous books have been translated into over twenty languages. Those available in English are, non-fiction: *How to Read Donald Duck* (with Armand Mattelart), 1971, *The Empire's Old Clothes*, 1983, and *Some Write to the Future*, 1991; the novels *Widows*, 1983, *The Last Song of Manuel Sendero*, 1986, *Mascara* 1988, *Hard Rain*, 1990; a collection of short stories, *My House is On Fire*, 1990; *Last Waltz in Santiago and Other Poems of Exile and Disappearance*, 1988; and the plays, *Widows*, *Reader* and *Death and the Maiden*. Research Professor of Literature and Latin American Studies at Duke University, Dorfman is a regular contributor to *The New York Times*, *The Los Angeles Times*, *The Nation*, *The Village Voice* and many other papers worldwide. He lives with his wife and two sons in Durham, North Carolina, and in Santiago, Chile. He is presently working on a new novel and a book of essays, *Missing Continents*.

Some opinions on his work:

'One of the most important voices coming out of Latin America.' (Salman Rushdie).

'Dorfman has assumed the mantle from the late poet Pablo Neruda as Chile's leading literary voice.' (*Los Angeles Times*).

'Of all the Latin American writers to come out of that explosion of creativity familiarly known as 'el boom', Ariel Dorfman is the one whose work I love best . . . He pushed the outer limit of the fictional envelope as daringly and imaginatively as Julio Cortazar and Gabriel Garcia Marquez, but what . . . makes Dorfman's books especially appealing is the humanism of his vision.' (Wendy Smith, *Cleveland Plain Dealer*).

Characters

PAULINA SALAS, around forty years old.
GERARDO ESCOBAR, her husband, a lawyer, around forty-five.
ROBERTO MIRANDA, a doctor, around fifty.

The time is the present and the place, a country that is probably Chile, but could be any country that has given itself a democratic government just after a long period of dictatorship.

The author would like to thank Linda Brandon and the ICA for bringing the play to the attention of the British public.

This text went to press before the opening night on the Main Stage of the Royal Court Theatre and may therefore differ slightly from the play as performed.

ACT ONE

Scene One

Sound of the sea. After midnight.
The ESCOBAR's *beach house. A terrace and an ample*
living/dining-room where dinner is laid out on a table with
two chairs. On a sideboard is a cassette-recorder and a lamp.
Window walls between the terrace and the front room, with
curtains blowing in the wind. A door from the terrace leading
to a bedroom. PAULINA SALAS *is seated in a chair on the*
terrace, as if she were drinking in the light of the moon. The
sound of a faraway car can be heard. She hurriedly stands up,
goes to the other room, looks out the window, crouches, and as
the headlights of the car sweep the living-room, she can be seen
rolled into a foetus-like position. The car brakes, its motor still
running, the lights blasting her. She goes to the sideboard,
takes out a gun, stops when the motor is taken off and she
hears GERARDO's *voice.*

GERARDO (*voice off*). You sure you won't come in?
(*Muffled reply.*) . . . But we must get together before I
leave. I'm leaving . . . Monday. Let's make it Sunday?
(*Muffled reply.*) . . . My wife makes a margarita that
will make your hair stand on end . . . I really want
you to know how much I appreciate . . . (*Muffled*
reply.) See you on Sunday then. (*He laughs.*)

PAULINA *hides the gun away. She stands behind the*
curtains. The car drives off, the lights sweeping the room
again. GERARDO *enters.*

GERARDO. Paulina? Love? God, it's dark.

He sees PAULINA *hidden behind the curtains. He switches*
on a light. She slowly comes out from the curtains.

Are you . . . ? What're you doing there like that?
Sorry I took this long to . . . I . . .

PAULINA (*agitated*). Who was it?

GERARDO. It's just that I . . .

PAULINA. Who brought you?

GERARDO. . . . had an – no, don't worry, it wasn't
anything serious. It's just that the car – luckily a man
stopped – just a flat tyre. Paulina, I can't see a thing
without . . .

He puts on another lamp and sees the table set.

Oh, love, look – it must've got cold, and you must
have –

PAULINA (*very calm, till the end of the scene*). We can
heat it up. As long as we've got something to
celebrate, that is.

Brief pause.

You do have something to celebrate, Gerardo, don't
you?

GERARDO. That depends on you.

Pause. He takes an enormous nail out of his jacket pocket.

You know what this is? This is the son of a bitch that
gave me a flat. And do you know what any normal
man does when he gets a flat? He goes to the boot
and he gets out the spare. If the spare isn't flat too,
that is. If his wife happened to remember to fix the
spare, right?

PAULINA. His wife. Always got to be the wife who has
to fix everything. You were supposed to fix the
spare.

GERARDO. I'm really not in the mood for arguing, but
we had agreed that . . .

PAULINA. You were supposed to fix the spare. I take
care of the house and you take care of –

GERARDO. You don't want help but afterwards
you . . .

PAULINA. – the car at least.

GERARDO. . . . afterwards you complain.

PAULINA. I never complain.

GERARDO. This is an absurd discussion. What're we fighting about? I've already forgotten what we . . .

PAULINA. We're not fighting, darling. You accused me of not fixing your spare . . .

GERARDO. *My* spare?

PAULINA. – and I told you quite sweetly that I –

GERARDO. Hold it right there. That you didn't fix the spare, *our* spare, that's open to discussion, but there is another little matter. The jack.

PAULINA. What jack?

GERARDO. Precisely. What jack? Where did you put the car jack? You know, to jack the –

PAULINA. You need a jack to hold up the car? And what are your strong arms for, my dear?

GERARDO (*embracing her*). For this.

Brief pause as they hug.

Do you know why you can afford to be so exasperating?

PAULINA. I can guess, but I'd rather you told me.

GERARDO. Because you know that the more you exasperate me, the more I love you. But what the hell did you do with the jack?

PAULINA. I gave it to Mother.

GERARDO (*letting go of her*). To your mother? You gave it to your mother?

PAULINA. Well, lent it to her, yes.

GERARDO. And may I know why?

PAULINA. You may. Because she needed it.

GERARDO. Whereas I, of course, we don't. You just can't – darling, you simply cannot do this sort of thing.

PAULINA. Mother was driving down south and really needed it. You can always . . .

GERARDO. Get lost.

PAULINA. No.

GERARDO. Yes. I get a telegram. The President wants
to see me. I have to leave for the city immediately for
the most important meeting of my whole life and on
my way back this son of a bitch of a nail is lying in
wait for me – and there I was on the road, in urgent
need of what any normal man would find in the boot
of his car – a spare and a jack. Paulina, I don't know
if you can get it into your pretty little head that . . .

PAULINA. My pretty little head knew that you'd find
someone to help you out. Who was it? Was she also
pretty?

GERARDO. I already said it was a man.

PAULINA. You said nothing of the sort.

GERARDO. Why do you always have to suppose there's
a woman . . .

PAULINA. Why indeed? I just can't imagine why.

Brief pause.

The man who . . . ? Was he nice?

GERARDO. Terrific guy. Mind you, if it had been
Count Dracula in person, I'd still have been grateful.

PAULINA. Well, there you are, you see. You always
manage to fix things up so that everything turns out
all right for you. But with Mother. If she had a flat
tyre you can be sure it really would be Count Dracula
who'd stop, you know how she attracts the weird
ones, she's like a magnet . . .

GERARDO. You can't imagine how ecstatic it makes me
to think of your mother exploring the south with my
jack, free of all worries, whilst I'm stuck on the
motorway for hours –

PAULINA. No exaggerating now . . .

GERARDO. Forty-five minutes. Forty-five. Road full of
weekend people racing for the coast. The cars passed
by as if I didn't exist. You know what I began to do?
I began to move my arms around like a windmill to
see if – but not a soul. What happened to ordinary

solidarity in this country? Lucky for me, this man –
Roberto Miranda – I invited him over for a –

PAULINA. I heard you.

GERARDO. How's Sunday?

PAULINA. Sunday's fine.

Brief pause.

GERARDO. As we're going back Monday. At least I
am. And I thought you might want to come with me,
shorten these holidays . . .

PAULINA. So the President named you?

Brief pause.

GERARDO. He did.

PAULINA. The peak of your career.

GERARDO. I wouldn't call it the peak. I am, after all,
the youngest of those he named, right?

PAULINA. Right. When you're Minister of Justice in a
few years' time, that'll be the peak, huh?

GERARDO. That certainly doesn't depend on me.

PAULINA. Did you tell him that?

GERARDO. Who?

PAULINA. Your Good Samaritan.

GERARDO. You mean Roberto Miranda? I hardly
know the man. Besides, I haven't decided yet if I
should . . .

PAULINA. You've decided.

GERARDO. I said I'd need a day or so, that I felt
extremely honoured but that I needed . . .

PAULINA. You said that to the President?

GERARDO. To the President. That I needed time to
think it over.

PAULINA. I don't see what you have to think over.
You've made your decision, Gerardo, you know you
have. It's what you've been working for all these
years, why pretend that . . .

GERARDO. Because first – first you have to say yes.

PAULINA. Well then: yes.

GERARDO. That's not the yes I need.

PAULINA. It's the only yes I've got.

GERARDO. I've heard others.

Brief pause.

If I were to accept, I must know I can count on you, that you don't feel . . . If you were to have a relapse, it could leave me . . .

PAULINA. Vulnerable, yes, it could leave you vulnerable. Stripped. You'd have to take care of me all over again.

GERARDO. That's unfair.

Brief pause.

Are you criticising me because I take care of you?

PAULINA. And that's what you told the President, that your wife might have problems with . . .

Pause.

GERARDO. He doesn't know. Nobody knows. Not even your mother knows.

PAULINA. There are people who know.

GERARDO. I'm not talking about those sort of people. Nobody in the new government knows. I'm talking about the fact that we never made it public, as you never – as we never denounced the things that they – what they . . .

PAULINA. Only if the result was death?

GERARDO. Paulina, I'm sorry, what do you – ?

PAULINA. This Commission you're named to. Doesn't it only investigate cases that ended in death?

GERARDO. It's appointed to investigate human rights' violations that ended in death or the presumption of death, yes.

PAULINA. Only the most serious cases?

GERARDO. The idea is that if we can cast light on the worst crimes, other abuses will come to light.

PAULINA. Only the most serious?

GERARDO. Those beyond redemption.

PAULINA. Only those beyond redemption, huh?

GERARDO. I don't like to talk about this, Paulina.

PAULINA. I don't like to talk about it either.

GERARDO. But we'll have to talk about it, won't we, you and I? If I'm going to spend the next few months listening to relatives and eyewitnesses and survivors – and each time I come back home I – and you wouldn't want me to keep all that to myself. And what if you . . . If you . . .

He takes her in his arms.

If you knew how much I love you. If you knew how it still hurts me.

Brief pause.

PAULINA (*fiercely holding on to him*). Yes. Yes. Yes. Is that the yes that you wanted?

GERARDO. That's the yes that I wanted.

PAULINA. Find out what happened. Find out everything. Promise me that that you'll find everything that . . .

GERARDO. Everything. Everything we can. We'll go as far as we . . . (*Pause.*) As we're . . .

PAULINA. Allowed.

GERARDO. Limited, let's say we're limited. But within those limits there is so much we can do . . . We'll publish our conclusions. There will be an official report. What happened will be established objectively, so no one will ever be able to deny it, so that our country will never again live through those excesses . . .

PAULINA. And then?

GERARDO. I don't understand.

PAULINA. You hear the relatives of the victims, you denounce the crimes, what happens to the criminals?

GERARDO. That depends on the Justices. The courts receive a copy of the evidence and the Justices proceed from there to –

PAULINA. The Justices? The same Justices who never intervened to save one life in seventeen years of dictatorship? Who never accepted a single *habeas corpus* ever? The Justices who said that nobody had been kidnapped, that if some poor woman's husband was missing it was because he was tired of her and had found another woman? What did you call them? Justices? Justices? Justices?

As she speaks, PAULINA *begins to laugh softly but with increasing hysteria.*

GERARDO. Paulina. That's enough. Paulina.

He takes her in his arms. She slowly calms down.

Silly. Silly girl, my silly little kitten. I'm so sorry. This is all my fault. I shouldn't have made so much of the tyre and that stupid car jack. It just struck me, suppose it was you out there, caught on the road, the lights screaming by you, nobody stopping, suppose you'd have been alone in the –

PAULINA. Someone would have stopped. Probably that same – Miranda?

GERARDO. Probably. Seems to be his mission in life. To rescue idiots and damsels in distress.

PAULINA. Sounds familiar.

GERARDO. Yes, we're kindred spirits.

PAULINA. Must be nice then.

GERARDO. Couldn't be nicer. If it weren't for him . . . I invited him to come for a drink on Sunday. Was that all right?

PAULINA. Sunday's fine. I was frightened. I heard a car. When I looked it wasn't yours.

GERARDO. But there was no danger.

PAULINA. No.

Brief pause.

Gerardo. You already said yes to the President, didn't you? The truth, Gerardo. Or are you going to start your work in the Commission with a lie?

GERARDO. I didn't want to hurt you.

PAULINA. You told the President you accepted, didn't you? Before you asked me? Didn't you? I need the truth, Gerardo.

GERARDO. Yes. I told him I'd do it. Yes.
Before asking you.

Lights go down.

Scene Two

One hour later. Nobody on stage. Only the moonlight, weaker than before, coming in through the windows. Dinner has been cleared away. Sound of the sea beyond. The sound of a car approaching. Then the headlights light up the living-room, are switched off, a car door is opened and closed. Someone knocks on the door, first timidly, then stronger. We hear the voices of PAULINA *and* GERARDO *from their bedroom.*

PAULINA (*voice off, whispering, terrorised*). Don't go.

GERARDO. Don't be silly. Nothing's going to happen, love.

A lamp is switched on from offstage and is immediately switched off.

PAULINA. They're coming for me, they're coming for me because I told you, because I didn't –

GERARDO. Easy, love.

The knocking on the door gets more insistent.

No one is coming to get you. No one knows –

PAULINA. Be careful. Promise me.

GERARDO. Nothing is going to – all right, all right, love, I'll be careful.

GERARDO *comes into the living-room in his pyjamas from the bedroom. He switches on the lamp.*

I'm coming, I'm coming.

He goes to the door and opens it. ROBERTO MIRANDA *is outside.*

Oh, it's you. Lord, you scared the life out of me.

ROBERTO. I'm really so sorry for this intrusion. I thought you'd still be up.

GERARDO. You must excuse me – do come in.

ROBERTO *enters the house.*

It's just that we are still not accustomed.

ROBERTO. Accustomed?

GERARDO. To democracy. Someone knocks on your door at midnight and is it a friend or one of –

PAULINA *edges out onto the terrace from where she will be able to hear the men but not see or be seen by them.*

ROBERTO. One of these sons of bitches?

GERARDO. And my wife has . . . she's been a bit nervous and . . . So you'll understand that – you'll have to forgive her if she doesn't . . . And if we lower our voices a little . . .

ROBERTO. Say no more, no more, it's my fault, I just thought . . .

GERARDO. Please sit down, please do . . .

ROBERTO. . . . that I'd stop by for a short visit to . . . Okay, but just a minute, no more than – but you must be asking yourself why this sudden visit . . . Well, you know when I drove on to our own beach-house, I don't know if you remember that I had the radio on, you may remember that . . .

GERARDO. Excuse me, would you like a drink? Sunday you can have one of my wife's famous margaritas, but I do possess a Cognac from the duty free that I –

PAULINA *edges nearer and listens.*

ROBERTO. No, thanks, I . . . Well, a teensy weensy bit. So I had the radio on and . . . all of a sudden, it hit me. I heard your name on the news, the list of names the President's chosen for his Investigating Commission, and they say Gerardo Escobar, and I said to myself that sounds familiar, but where, who, and it kept going round in my head, and when I reached our house I realised who it was. And I also remembered we'd put your spare tyre in the boot of my car and that tomorrow you'd need it patched up and also . . . the real real truth is, you want to know the truth? –

GERARDO. Nothing but.

ROBERTO. I thought to myself – this man is doing something really essential, crucial for the honour of the nation – so the country can come together again, can have some reconciliation, shut the door on the divisions and hatreds of the past and I've got his spare tyre. I thought here's the last weekend that he's going to be free of worries for – for who knows how many more months, right, because you're going to have to go up and down this land of ours listening to thousands of people . . . Don't tell me that this won't be the last weekend that you're going to . . .

GERARDO. That's certainly true, but I wouldn't go so far as to –

ROBERTO. So I thought the least I can do is drive over. Or find a garage for him. I mean, who has a phone out here. So he won't lose his time, I thought to myself, valuable time which could –

GERARDO. You're making me feel like a saint.

ROBERTO. No. This is straight from the heart. This Commission will help us close a very painful chapter in our history, and here I am, alone this weekend. So I said to myself, Dr Miranda to the rescue, this is a job for you, we've all got to help out – it may be a teensy weensy gesture but –

GERARDO. Tomorrow would have been fine.

ROBERTO. And you get up early. No car outside. You get to your car – no spare. Then you have to set out

and find me. No, my good man, – and then I
thought what if I also take him to the garage
tomorrow and I find him a jack. Which reminds me
– what happened to your jack, did you find out
what –

GERARDO. My wife lent it to her mother.

ROBERTO. To her mother?

GERARDO. You know how women are . . .

ROBERTO (*laughing*). I know all too well. It's the
female soul. Utterly unpredictable. You know what
Nietzche once wrote? The female soul is never
entirely ours, we can never entirely possess it. Or
maybe he didn't write that. Though you can be sure
that old Nietzche would have if he'd been caught in
the roar of the weekend traffic without a jack.

GERARDO. And without a spare.

ROBERTO. And without a spare. Which clinches it – I
really must accompany you and we'll clean up the
whole operation in one morning . . .

GERARDO. I do feel that I am imposing upon your –

ROBERTO. I won't hear another word. I happen to
like helping people, – I'm a doctor, I think I told
you, didn't I? – But don't imagine I only help
important people.

GERARDO. If you had known what you were getting
into you'd have pushed your foot down on the
accelerator full blast, huh?

ROBERTO (*laughing*). Full blast. No, seriously, it's no
trouble at all. In fact, it's an honour. In fact that's
why I came here tonight, really. To congratulate you.
You are exactly what this country needs, to be able to
know the truth once and for all . . .

GERARDO. What the country needs is justice, but if we
can establish at least part of the truth . . .

ROBERTO. Just what I was about to say. Even if we
can't put these people on trial, even if they're covered
by this amnesty they gave themselves – at least we'll
see their names in print.

GERARDO. Those names are to be kept secret. The Commission is not supposed to identify the authors of crimes or –

ROBERTO. In this country everything finally comes out into the open. Their children, their grandchildren, is it true that you did this, you did what they're accusing you of, and they'll have to lie. They'll say it's slander, it's a communist conspiracy, some such nonsense, but the truth will be written all over them, and their children, their very own children, will feel sorrow for them, disgust and sorrow. It's not like putting them in gaol, but . . .

GERARDO. Maybe some day . . .

ROBERTO. Maybe if the citizens of this country get angry enough we may even be able to revoke the amnesty.

GERARDO. You know that's not possible.

ROBERTO. I'm for killing the whole bunch of them, but I can see that . . .

GERARDO. I'm afraid I have to disagree with you, Roberto, because in my opinion the death penalty has never solved –

ROBERTO. Then we're going to have to disagree, my friend. There are some people who simply don't deserve to be alive, but what I was really getting at was that you're going to have quite a problem . . .

GERARDO. More than one. For starters, the Army is going to fight the Commission all the way. They've told the President it would be dangerous, yes, dangerous, because it will open old wounds. Thank God, the President didn't get cold feet, but we all know these people are ready to jump on us at the slightest mistake we make . . .

ROBERTO. Well, that was exactly my point, when you said that the names wouldn't be known, published, when you – that got me to thinking that maybe you're right, maybe we'll finally never know who these people really were, don't you see that they form a sort of . . .

GERARDO. Mafia.

ROBERTO. Mafia, yes, a secret brotherhood, nobody
gives out names and they cover each others' backs.
The Armed Forces aren't going to allow their men to
give testimony to your Commission and if you people
call them in they'll just ignore your summons.
Whatever they please . . . they've got the guns . . .
Maybe I take back what I said about the children. It
was a nice dream.

GERARDO. The President told me – and this is strictly
between us –

ROBERTO. Strictly.

GERARDO. He told me that there are people who are
ready to make statements, just so long as their
confidentiality is guaranteed. And once people start
talking, once the confessions, the names will pour out
like water. Like you said: in this country we end up
knowing everything. So your dream may still . . .

ROBERTO. I wish I could share your optimism. I'm
afraid there are things we'll never know.

GERARDO. We're limited, my friend, but not that
limited. At the very least we can expect some sort of
moral sanction, that's the least . . . As we can't expect
justice from the courts . . .

ROBERTO. I hope to God you're right. But it's getting
late. Good Lord, it's two o'clock. Look, I'll be back
to pick you up tomorrow, let's say at – how about
nine?

GERARDO. Why don't you stay over unless you've got
someone waiting for you back at your . . .

ROBERTO. Not a soul.

GERARDO. Well, if you're alone.

ROBERTO. Not alone. My wife and kids have gone off
to Disneyland of all places. God, I hate Disneyland
and anyway I've got patients to look after.

GERARDO. Not at your beach house you don't. So why
don't you stay over.

ROBERTO. It's very kind of you but I like being by myself, watching the waves, listening to my music. Look, I came to help, not to be a bother. I'll be back tomorrow, say at —

GERARDO. I won't hear of it. You're staying. You're what? You're half an hour away?

ROBERTO. It's around forty minutes by the coast road, but if I —

GERARDO. Not another word. The spare room's made up. Paulina will be delighted. You'll see the breakfast she'll make for us. Eggs. French bread. Melon and ham. You like melon and ham?

ROBERTO. I love melon and ham.

GERARDO. You can devour as much melon and ham as you want. And then we'll go and get the car.

ROBERTO. Done. And the real real truth is that I am incredibly tired . . .

PAULINA *quickly returns, through the terrace, to her bedroom.*

GERARDO. I wonder if there's anything else you might . . . ? A toothbrush is really the only thing I think I can't offer you . . .

ROBERTO. One never shares one's toothbrush, my friend. Or one's woman.

GERARDO. No . . .

ROBERTO. Goodnight.

Both GERARDO *and* ROBERTO *exit in different directions to their respective bedrooms. A brief pause: silence and moonlight.*

GERARDO (*voice off*). Paulina, love . . . That doctor who helped me up on the road, he's staying the night. Love? He's staying because tomorrow he's going to help me pick up the car. Darling, are you listening?

PAULINA (*off, as if half-asleep*). Yes, my love.

GERARDO (*voice off*). He's a friend. So don't be

frightened. Tomorrow you can make us a nice
breakfast . . .
Only the sound of the sea in the semi-darkness.

Scene Three

*A short time later. A cloud passes over the moon. The sound of
the sea grows, then recedes. Silence.*

PAULINA (*voice off, whispering*). Gerardo? Gerardo?

*There is no answer. PAULINA comes into the living-room.
By the light of the moon she can be seen going to the drawer
and taking out the gun. And some vague articles of clothing
which appear to be stockings. She stops. She thinks she hears
GERARDO move in the bedroom. She is dressed.*

Love . . . ? Love?

*She crosses the living-dining-room to the entrance to
ROBERTO's bedroom. She waits for an instant, listening.
She goes into the bedroom. A few moments pass. We hear a
confusing, muffled sound, followed by a sort of cry.
Then silence.
In the half-light we see her come out of the room. She goes
back to her own bedroom door. She opens it, takes a key
from the inside of the door, locks it. She returns to the spare
bedroom. We see her dragging something which resembles a
body but we can't be sure. She moves a chair and hoists the
body onto it, ties it to the chair. She goes into the spare
room, returns with what seems to be ROBERTO's jacket,
takes a set of car keys from it. She starts to leave the house.
Stops. Turns back to look at the body which is now clearly
that of ROBERTO. She takes off her panties, stuffs them
into ROBERTO's mouth.*
PAULINA *leaves the house. We hear the sound of
ROBERTO's car. When the car's headlights are turned on,
they sweep the scene and that stark brutal shot of light
clearly reveals* ROBERTO MIRANDA *tied with ropes to
one of the chairs, totally unconscious, and with his mouth
gagged. The car leaves. Darkness.*

Scene Four

Before dawn.
ROBERTO *opens his eyes. He tries to get up and realises
that he is tied. He begins to roll over and desperately try to
free himself.* PAULINA *is sitting in front of him with her
gun.* ROBERTO *looks at her with a terrorised expression in
his eyes.*

PAULINA (*very calm*). Good morning, Dr . . . Miranda,
isn't it? Dr Miranda.

*She shows him the gun and points it playfully in his
direction.*

I had a chum from the University, name of Miranda,
Maria Elena Miranda, you wouldn't be related to the
Mirandas of San Esteban, would you? She had quite a
mind. A marvellous retentive memory, we used to
call her our little encyclopaedia. I have no idea what
became of her. She probably finished her medical
studies, became a doctor, just like you.
I didn't get my diploma . . . I didn't get too far with
my studies, Dr Miranda. Let's see if you can guess
why I didn't get my diploma, I'm pretty sure that it
won't take a colossal effort of the imagination on
your part to guess why.
Luckily there was Gerardo. He was – well, I wouldn't
exactly say he was waiting for me – but let's say that
he still loved me, so I never had to go back to the
University. Lucky for me, because I felt – well,
phobia wouldn't be the right word, a certain
apprehension – about medicine. I wasn't so sure
about my chosen profession. But life is never over till
it's over, as they say. That's why I'm wondering
whether it might not be a good idea to sign up again
– you know, ask that I be readmitted. I read the
other day, now that the military aren't in charge
anymore, that the University has begun to allow the
students who were kicked out to apply for
readmittance.
But here I am chatting away when I'm supposed to
make breakfast, aren't I, a nice breakfast? Now you
like – let's see, ham with mayonnaise, wasn't that it?
Ham with mayonnaise sandwiches. We haven't got
mayonnaise, but we do have ham. Gerardo also likes

ham. I'll get to know your other tastes. Sorry about
the mayonnaise. I hope you don't mind that this must
remain, for the moment, a monologue. You'll have
your say, Doctor, you can be sure of that. I just don't
want to remove this – gag, you call it, don't you? – at
least not till Gerardo wakes up. But I should be
getting him up. Did I tell you I phoned the garage
from the call box? They'll be here soon.

She goes to the bedroom door, unlocks it, opens it.

The real real truth is that you look slightly bored.

Takes a cassette out of her pocket.

I took this out of your car – I took the liberty – what
if we listen to some Schubert while I make breakfast,
a nice breakfast, Doctor? 'Death and the Maiden'?

*She puts it into the cassette-player. We begin to hear
Schubert's quartet 'Death and the Maiden'.*

D'you know how long it's been since I last listened to
this quartet? If it's on the radio, I switch it off, I even
try not to go out much, though Gerardo has all these
social events he's got to attend and if they ever name
him Minister we're going to live running around
shaking hands and smiling at perfect strangers, but I
always pray they won't put on Schubert. One night
we were dining with – they were extremely important
people, and our hostess happened to put Schubert
on, a piano sonata, and I thought, do I switch it off
or do I leave, but my body decided for me, I felt
extremely ill right then and there and Gerardo had
to take me home, so we left them there listening to
Schubert and nobody knew what had made me ill, so
I pray they won't play that anywhere I go, any
Schubert at all, strange isn't it, when he used to be,
and I would say, yes I really would say, he's still my
favourite composer, such a sad, noble sense of life.
But I always promised myself a time would come to
recover him, bring him back from the grave so to
speak, and just sitting here listening to him with you
I know that I was right, that I'm – so many things
that are going to change from now on, right? To
think I was on the verge of throwing my whole
Schubert collection out, crazy!

(*Raising her voice, to* GERARDO.) Isn't this quartet marvellous, my love.

(*To* ROBERTO.) And now I'll be able to listen to my Schubert again, even go to a concert like we used to. Did you know that Schubert was homosexual? But of course you do, you're the one who kept repeating it over and over in my ear over and over again while you played 'Death and the Maiden'. Is this the very cassette, Doctor, or do you buy a new one every year to keep the sound pure?

GERARDO *enters from the bedroom, still sleepy.*

Good morning, my darling. Sorry breakfast isn't ready yet.

Upon seeing GERARDO, ROBERTO *makes desperate efforts to untie himself.* GERARDO *watches the scene with total astonishment.*

GERARDO. Paulina! What is this? What in the name of . . . Roberto . . . Dr Miranda.

He moves towards ROBERTO.

PAULINA. Don't touch him.

GERARDO. What?

PAULINA (*threatening him with the gun*). Don't touch him.

GERARDO. What the hell is going on here, what kind of madness is –

PAULINA. It's him.

GERARDO. Put . . . put that gun down.

PAULINA. It's him.

GERARDO. Who?

PAULINA. It's the man.

GERARDO. What man?

PAULINA. The doctor.

GERARDO. What doctor?

PAULINA. The doctor who played Schubert.

GERARDO. The doctor who played Schubert.

PAULINA. That doctor.

GERARDO. How do you know?

PAULINA. His voice.

GERARDO. You told me – what you told me was all through those weeks, you said –

PAULINA. I was blindfolded, yes. But I could hear.

GERARDO. You're ill.

PAULINA. I'm not ill.

GERARDO. You're ill.

PAULINA. All right then, I am. But I can be ill and recognise a voice. Besides, when we lose one of our faculties, the others compensate, they get sharper. Right, Dr Miranda?

GERARDO. A vague memory of someone's voice is not proof of anything.

PAULINA. It's his voice. I recognised it as soon as he came in here last night. The way he laughed. Certain phrases he used.

GERARDO. But that's not . . .

PAULINA. It may be a teensy weensy thing, but it's enough for me. During all these years not an hour has passed that I haven't heard it, that same voice, next to me, next to my ear, that voice mixed with saliva, you think I'd forget a voice like his?

Imitating the voice of ROBERTO, *then of a man.*

'Give her a bit more. This bitch can take a bit more. Give it to her.'
'You sure, Doctor? What if the cunt dies on us?'
'She's not even near fainting. Give it to her, up another notch.'

GERARDO. Paulina. I'm asking you to give me that gun.

PAULINA. No.

GERARDO. We can't talk with that pointing at me.

PAULINA. On the contrary, we can only talk with this
pointing at you. If I put it down you'll use your
superior strength to win the argument.

GERARDO. Paulina, I want you to know that what you
are doing is going to have serious consequences.

PAULINA. Serious, huh? Beyond redemption?

GERARDO. Yes, it could be. Beyond redemption. Dr
Miranda, I have to ask your forgiveness for –

PAULINA. Don't you dare ask that from that piece of
shit.

GERARDO. Untie him, Paulina.

PAULINA. No.

GERARDO. Then I will.

He moves towards ROBERTO. *Suddenly, a shot from*
PAULINA's *gun rings out. It's clear that she does not
know how to fire the weapon, because she is as surprised as
both men are, recoiling from the shot.* GERARDO *takes a
step backward and* ROBERTO *looks desperate.*

PAULINA. Oh my God!

GERARDO. Don't fire that thing again, Pau. Give me
that gun. (*Silence.*) You can't do this.

PAULINA. When are you going to stop telling me what
I can and can't do. 'You can't do this, you can do
this, you can't do this.' I did it.

GERARDO. You did this to this man, whose only fault
that we know of – the only thing you can accuse him
of in front of a court of justice –

PAULINA *laughs derisively.*

– yes, a court, of justice, yes, however corrupt, venal,
cowardly – the only thing you could accuse him of is
of stopping on a motorway to help someone who was
in trouble, and bring me home and then offer to –

PAULINA. I almost forgot. The garage man will be
here any minute.

GERARDO. What?

PAULINA. When I went to hide your Good

Samaritan's car early this morning, I stopped at a call box and rang the garage. So you better get dressed, he'll be here soon.

GERARDO. Please, Paulina, could we try something else? Could we start being reasonable.

PAULINA. You be reasonable. They never did anything to you.

GERARDO. Of course they did things – but we're not competing for some horror prize here, damn it. Even if this man was the doctor of those terrible events – he isn't, there's no reason why he should be, but let's say he was – even in that case, you have no right in law or otherwise to do what you have done. Paulina, think of the consequences, try to –

The motor of a truck is heard outside. PAULINA *runs to the door, half opens it and shouts out.*

PAULINA. He's coming, he's coming.

She shuts the door, locks it, closes the curtains and looks at GERARDO.

Here he is. Get dressed, quick. Go with the garage man. He'll take you to the car and fix it. The spare tyre's outside. I also took his jack.

GERARDO. You're stealing his jack?

PAULINA. That way Mother can keep ours.

Brief pause.

GERARDO. Have you thought I could go to the police?

PAULINA. I doubt you'd do that. You believe too much in your own powers of persuasion. Besides you know that if the police do show their noses here I'll put a bullet straight through this man's head, you know that, don't you? And then I'll put the gun into my mouth and pull the trigger.

GERARDO. Oh my baby, my baby. You're – unrecognisable. How can you possibly be like this, talk like this?

PAULINA. Explain to my husband, Dr Miranda, what you did to me so I would be this – crazy.

GERARDO. So – what exactly do you plan to do?

PAULINA. Not me. You and me. We're going to put him on trial, Gerardo, this doctor. Right here. Today. Or is your famous Investigating Commission going to do it?

Lights go down.

ACT TWO

Scene One

Midday.
ROBERTO *is still in the same position,* PAULINA *with her back to him, looking outwards to the window and the sea, rocking herself gently as she speaks to him.*

PAULINA. And when they let me go – d'you know where I went? I couldn't go home to my parents – they were so pro-military, I'd see Mother only once in a long while. – Isn't this bizarre, that I should be telling you all this as if you were my confessor, when there are things I've never told Gerardo, or my sister, certainly not my mother. She'd die if she knew what I've really got in my head. Whereas I can tell you exactly what I feel, what I felt when they let me go. That night . . . well, you don't need me to describe what state I was in, you gave me a quite thorough inspection before I was released, didn't you. We're rather cosy here, aren't we, like this? Like two old pensioners sitting on a bench in the sun.

ROBERTO *makes a gesture, as if he wanted to speak or untie himself.*

Hungry? Things aren't that bad. You'll just have to be patient until Gerardo comes.

(*Imitating a man's voice.*) 'You hungry? You wanna eat? I'll give you something to eat, sweet cunt, I'll give you something really filling so you can forget you're hungry.'

(*Her own voice.*) None of you knew about Gerardo, did you? – I never breathed his name. Your – your colleagues, they'd ask me, of course. 'With that twat, little lady, don't tell me you haven't got someone to fuck you, huh? Come on, just tell us who's been fucking you, little lady.' But I never gave them Gerardo's name. Strange how things turn out. If I had mentioned Gerardo, he wouldn't have been named to any Commission, but would have been one of the names that some other lawyer was investigating. And I would be in front of that Commission to tell them how I met Gerardo – in fact I met him just after the military coup, helping people seek asylum in embassies – saving lives with Gerardo, smuggling people out of the country so they wouldn't be killed. I was wild and fearless, willing to do anything, I can't believe that I hadn't got an ounce of fear in my whole body at that time. But where was I? Oh yes – that night they let me go, well, I went to Gerardo's house, I knocked on the door, long quiet knocks, over and over, just like you did last night, and when Gerardo finally answered, he looked agitated, his hair was dishevelled –

The sound of a car outside. Then a car door opening and closing. PAULINA *goes to the table and takes the gun in her hand.* GERARDO *enters.*

How did it go? Fix the tyre?

GERARDO. Paulina, you are going to listen to me.

PAULINA. Of course I'm going to listen to you. Don't I always?

GERARDO. I want you to sit down and I want you to really listen to me.

PAULINA *sits down.*

You know that I have spent a good part of my life defending the law. If there was one thing that revolted me in the past regime –

PAULINA. You can call them fascists . . .

GERARDO. Don't interrupt. If something revolted me about them it was that they accused so many men and women, that they forged evidence and ignored evidence and did not give the accused any chance of defending themselves, so even if this man committed genocide on a daily basis, he has the right to defend himself.

PAULINA. But I have no intention of denying him that right, Gerardo. I'll give you all the time you need to speak to your client, in private. I was just waiting for you to come back, that's all, so we could begin this in an orderly fashion.

She gestures to GERARDO, *who takes the gag off* ROBERTO. *Then she indicates the cassette-recorder.*

You should know, Doctor, that everything you say will be recorded here.

GERARDO. My God, Paulina, shut up! Let him say what he . . .

Brief pause. PAULINA *switches on the recorder.*

ROBERTO (*coughs, then in a rough, hoarse voice*). Water.

GERARDO. What?

PAULINA. He wants water, Gerardo.

GERARDO *rushes to fill a glass with water and brings it to* ROBERTO, *giving it to him to drink.* ROBERTO *drinks it down noisily.*

PAULINA. Nothing like good fresh water, eh, Doctor? Beats drinking your own piss.

ROBERTO. Escobar. This is inexcusable. I will never forgive you as long as I live.

PAULINA. Hold on, hold on. Stop right there, Doctor. Let's see if this thing is working.

She presses some buttons and then we hear ROBERTO's *voice.*

ROBERTO'S VOICE FROM THE CASSETTE. Escobar. This is inexcusable. I will never forgive you as long as I live.

PAULINA'S VOICE FROM THE CASSETTE. Hold on, hold on. Stop right there, Doctor, Let's see –

PAULINA *stops the recorder.*

PAULINA. Ready. It's recording everything marvellously. We already have a statement about forgiveness. It is Dr Miranda's opinion that it is inexcusable – that he could never forgive as long as he lives – tying someone up for a few hours, holding that person without the right to speak for a few hours. Agreed. More?

She presses another button.

ROBERTO. I do not know you, madame. I have never seen you in my life before. But I can tell you this: you are extremely ill, almost prototypically schizoid. But you, Escobar, your case is different. You're a lawyer, a defender of human rights, a man who has been persecuted by the former military government, as I was myself, and you are responsible for what you do and what you must do is untie me immediately. I want you to know that every minute that passes makes you more of an accomplice to this abuse and that you will therefore have to pay the consequences of –

PAULINA (*puts the gun to his temple*). Are you threatening?

ROBERTO. I wasn't –

PAULINA. Threatening, yes you are, but not in here. Let's get this clear, Doctor. Out there you bastards may still give the orders, you can veto our lives, but in here, I'm in command. Are we clear?

ROBERTO. I'm in pain.

PAULINA. I know.

ROBERTO. I must go to the bathroom.

PAULINA. Piss or shit?

GERARDO. My God, Paulina! Dr Miranda, she has never spoken like this in her life.

PAULINA. Come on, Doctor. Back or front?

ROBERTO. Standing up.

PAULINA. Untie his legs, Gerardo. I'll take him.

GERARDO. Of course you won't.

PAULINA. I'll do it. Don't look at me like that. It's not as if it's the first time he's taken his thing out in front of me, Gerardo. Come on, Doctor. Stand up. I don't want you pissing all over my floor.

GERARDO *unties the legs. Slowly, painfully,* ROBERTO *limps towards the bathroom, with* PAULINA *sticking the gun in his back.* GERARDO *takes off the cassette-recorder.* PAULINA *goes out with* ROBERTO. *After a few instants, we can hear the sounds of urination and then flushing. Meanwhile,* GERARDO *has been pacing nervously.* PAULINA *returns with* ROBERTO.

PAULINA. Tie him up again.

GERARDO *begins to tie up* ROBERTO's *legs.*

Tighter, Gerardo!

GERARDO. Paulina, this is intolerable. I must talk with you.

PAULINA. And who's stopping you?

GERARDO. Alone.

PAULINA. Why? The Doctor discussed everything in my presence, they –

GERARDO. I beg you darling, please, don't be so difficult. I want to talk to you where he can't hear us.

GERARDO *and* PAULINA *go out onto the terrace. During their conversation,* ROBERTO *slowly manages to loosen his leg bonds.*

What are you trying to do?

PAULINA. I already told you – put him on trial.

GERARDO. Put him on trial, what does that mean, put him on trial? We can't use their methods. We're different. To seek vengeance in this fashion is not –

PAULINA. This is not vengeance. I'm giving him all the guarantees he never gave me. Not one, him and his – colleagues.

GERARDO. And his – colleagues – are you going to kidnap them and bring them here and tie them up and . . .

PAULINA. I'd have to know their names for that, wouldn't I?

GERARDO. – and then you're going to . . .

PAULINA. Kill them? Kill him? As he didn't kill me, I think it wouldn't be fair to —

GERARDO. That's good to know. Paulina, because I'm warning you, you'd have to kill me first. I swear it.

PAULINA. Would you mind calming down? I haven't the slightest intention of killing him. And certainly not you . . . But as usual, you don't believe me.

GERARDO. But then, what are you going to do to him? You're going to — what?, — and all this because fifteen years ago someone . . .

PAULINA. Someone what? . . . what did they do to me, Gerardo. Say it.

Brief pause.

You never wanted to say it. Say it now. They . . . .

GERARDO. If you didn't say it, how was I going to?

PAULINA. Say it now.

GERARDO. I only know what you told me that first night, when . . .

PAULINA. They . . .

GERARDO. They . . .

PAULINA. Tell me, tell me.

GERARDO. They — tortured you. Now you say it.

PAULINA. They tortured me.
And what else? What else did they do to me, Gerardo?

GERARDO *goes to her, takes her in his arms.*

GERARDO (*whispering to her*). They raped you.

PAULINA. How many times?

GERARDO. More than once.

PAULINA. How many times?

GERARDO. You never said. You said you didn't count.

PAULINA. It's not true.

GERARDO. What's not true?

PAULINA. That I didn't count. I always kept count. I know how many times.

Brief pause.

And that night, Gerardo, when I came to you, when I started to tell you, you swore, I remember you said: 'Some day, my love, we're going to put these bastards on trial. Your eyes will be able to rove – I remember the exact phrase, because it seemed, poetic – your eyes will be able to rove over each one of their faces while they listen to your story. We'll do it, you'll see that we will.' So now, darling, tell me who do I go to now?

GERARDO. That was fifteen years ago.

PAULINA. Gerardo, do I go to your Commission now?

GERARDO. Mine? I don't think it will be mine much longer after today. I shall have to resign.

PAULINA. Always so melodramatic. And then your forehead gets all wrinkled up which makes you look ten years older. And then people will see your photograph in the newspaper and won't believe that you're the youngest member of the Commission.

GERARDO. Are you deaf? I just told you I'm going to have to resign.

PAULINA. I don't see why.

GERARDO. You don't see why, but all the rest of the country will see why, especially those who don't want any kind of investigation at all. A member of the President's Commission, who should be showing exemplary signs of moderation and equanimity –

PAULINA. We're going to suffocate from so much equanimity!

GERARDO. – and objectivity, that this very person has allowed an innocent human being to be bound and tormented in his house, without a shred of evidence against him admissible in a court of law.

PAULINA. What court of law?

GERARDO. Paulina, do you know how the newspapers that served the dictatorship, do you know how they'll use this episode to undermine and even wreck the Commission?

Brief pause.

Do you want these people back in power? Every minute that passes, every second, that you've got this poor man tied up, makes it harder for us. Free the man, Paulina. Apologise for the mistake and free him. I've spoken to him, politically he seems to be a man we can trust or so it –

PAULINA. Oh, my little man, you do fall for every trick in the book, don't you? But let's not waste . . . If you could just listen to me for a change, my love. I'm not trying to harm your career and I most certainly don't want to jeopardise the Commission. But you see the Commission only deals with the dead, with those who can't speak. And I can speak – it's been so long since I as much as whispered a word, even a breath of what I'm thinking, years living in terror of my own . . . but I'm not dead, I thought I was but I'm not and I can speak, – so for God's sake let me have my say and you go ahead with your Commission and believe me when I tell you that none of this will be made public.

GERARDO. The only way that will happen is if the man out there benevolently decides not to make the matter public. And anyway, I have to resign no matter what. The sooner, the better.

PAULINA. You'd have to resign even if no one knew about this?

GERARDO. Yes.

PAULINA. Because of your mad wife, who was mad because she stayed silent and is now mad because she suddenly began to speak?

GERARDO. Among other reasons, yes, that's so, if the truth still matters to you.

PAULINA. Oh it does, the real real truth.

Brief pause.

Hang on a sec.

She goes into the other room and discovers ROBERTO *about to free himself. When he sees her, he stops immediately.* PAULINA *ties him up again, while her voice assumes male tones.*

'Hey, don't you like our hospitality? Want to leave so soon, bitch? You're not going to have such a good time outside as you're having with me, sweetie. Tell me you'll miss me. At least tell me that.'

PAULINA *begins to pass her hands slowly up and down* ROBERTO'*s body, almost as if she were caressing it. Then she goes back to the bedroom.*

PAULINA. It's not only the voice I recognise, Gerardo. I also recognise the skin. And the smell. Gerardo. I recognise his skin.

Brief pause.

Suppose I was able to prove beyond a shadow of a doubt that this doctor of yours is guilty? Would you want me to set him free then?

GERARDO. Yes.
If he's guilty, more reason to let him go. Don't look at me like that. You want to scare these people and provoke them, Paulina, till they come back, make them so insecure that they come back to make sure we don't harm them – you want them back? Because that's what you're going to get. Imagine what would happen if everyone acted like you did. You satisfy your own personal passion, you punish on your own, while the other people in this country with scores of other problems who finally have a chance to solve some of them, those people can go screw themselves – the whole transition to democracy can go screw itself –

PAULINA. Nothing's going to happen to democracy! Nobody's even going to know!

GERARDO. The only way to be absolutely sure about that is to kill him and then we're both finished. Let him go, Paulina. For the good of the country, for our own good.

PAULINA. What about my good? What about me? Look at me.

GERARDO. Yes, look at you, love. You're still a prisoner, locked up with them, in that basement. For fifteen years you've done nothing with your life. Not a thing. Look at you, just when we've got the chance to start all over again . . . Isn't it time we – ?

PAULINA. – forgot? You're asking me to forget.

GERARDO. Free yourself from them, Paulina, that's what I'm asking.

PAULINA. And let him loose so he can come back in a few years' time?

GERARDO. So he won't come back ever again.

PAULINA. And we see him at the Tavelli and we smile at him, he introduces his lovely wife to us and we smile and we all shake hands and we comment on how warm it is this time of the year?

GERARDO. Basically yes, and start to live.

Brief pause.

PAULINA. Look, Gerardo, I suggest we reach a compromise.

GERARDO. I don't follow you.

PAULINA. You concede something, I concede something. Isn't that what this transition is all about? Compromise, negotiation. They let us have democracy, but they keep control of the economy and of the Armed Forces? The Commission can investigate the crimes but nobody is punished for them? There's freedom to say anything you want as long as you don't say everything you want?

Brief pause.

I propose that we reach an agreement. You want this man freed and I want – would you like to know what I want?

GERARDO. I'd love to know what you want.

PAULINA. When I heard his voice last night, the first thought that rushed through my head, what I've been thinking all these years, when you would catch me with a look that you said was – abstract, fleeting, right? – you know what I was thinking of? Doing to them, systematically, minute by minute, instrument by instrument, what they did to me. Specifically to him, to the doctor . . . Because the others were so vulgar, so – but he would play Schubert, he would talk about science, he even quoted Nietzche to me once.

GERARDO. Nietzche.

PAULINA. I was horrified at myself. That I should have such hatred in me, that I should want to do something like that to a defenceless human being, no matter how vile – but it was the only way to fall asleep at night, the only way of going out with you to cocktail parties in spite of the fact that I couldn't help asking myself if one of those present wasn't – perhaps not the exact same man, but one of those present might be . . . and so as not to go completely off my rocker and be able to deliver that Tavelli smile you say I'm going to have to continue to deliver – well, I would imagine pushing their head into a bucket of slime, or electricity, or when we would be making love and I could feel the possibility of an orgasm building, the very idea of currents going through my body would remind me and then – and then I had to simulate it, simulate it so you wouldn't know what I was thinking, so you wouldn't feel that it was your failure – oh Gerardo.

GERARDO. Oh, my love, my love.

PAULINA. So when I heard his voice, I thought the only thing I want is to have him raped, have somone fuck him, so that he should know just once what it is to . . . And as I can't – I thought that it was a sentence that you would have to carry out.

GERARDO. Don't go on, Paulina.

PAULINA. But then I told myself it could be difficult, after all you do need to have a certain degree of enthusiasm to –

GERARDO. Stop, Paulina.

PAULINA. So I asked myself if we couldn't use a broom handle. Yes, Gerardo, you know, a broom.

But I began to realise that wasn't what I really
wanted. And you know what conclusion I came to,
the only thing I really want?

Brief pause.

I want him to confess. I want him to sit in front of
that cassette-recorder and tell me what he did – not
just to me, everything, to everybody – and then have
him write it out in his own handwriting and sign it
and I would keep a copy forever – with all the
information, the names and data, all the details.
That's what I want.

GERARDO. He confesses and you let him go.

PAULINA. I let him go.

GERARDO. And you need nothing more from him?

PAULINA. Not a thing.

Brief pause.

Don't you see it's a way of protecting you, my love.
With Miranda's confession in my hand you'd be safe
on the Commission and he wouldn't dare send his
thugs to harm us because he'd know that the
confession would be all over the newspapers the next
day. Don't you see?

GERARDO. And you expect me to believe you that
you're going to let him go after he's confessed? Do
you expect him to believe that?

PAULINA. I don't see that either of you have an
alternative. Look, Gerardo, you need to make this
sort of scum afraid. Tell him I hid the car because
I'm getting ready to kill him. That the only way to
dissuade me is for him to confess. Tell him that
nobody knows he came last night, that nobody would
ever find him. For his sake, I hope you can convince
him.

GERARDO. Are you saying I have to convince him?

PAULINA. I'm saying it's a lot more pleasant than
having to fuck him.

GERARDO. There's a problem, Paulina. What do I do
if he has nothing to confess?

PAULINA. Tell him if he doesn't confess, I'll kill him.

GERARDO. But what if he's not guilty.

PAULINA. I'm in no hurry. Tell him I can wait months for him to confess.

GERARDO. Paulina, you're not listening to me. What can he confess if he's innocent?

PAULINA. If he's innocent? Then we're – then he's really screwed.

Lights go down.

Scene Two

Lunch. GERARDO *and* ROBERTO *sit at a table.*
ROBERTO *still tied, but this time with his hands in front.*
GERARDO *has just finished serving plates of soup.*
PAULINA *watches from the terrace. She can see but not hear them.* ROBERTO *and* GERARDO *remain for several silent instants looking at the food.*

GERARDO. You're not hungry, Dr Miranda?

ROBERTO. Roberto. My name is Roberto. Please treat me with the same familiarity as before. Maybe it will make me feel better.

GERARDO. I'd rather speak to you as if you were a client, Dr Miranda. That will help me out. I do think you should eat something.

ROBERTO. I'm not hungry.

GERARDO. Let me . . .

He fills a spoon with soup and feeds ROBERTO *as if he were a baby. During the conversation which follows, he is continually feeding* ROBERTO *and feeding himself.*

ROBERTO. She's mad. You'll have to excuse me for saying this, Gerardo, but your wife is mad, you know.

GERARDO. Bread?

ROBERTO. No, thanks.

Brief pause.

She should be receiving some sort of psychiatric treatment for –

GERARDO. You are her therapy, Doctor.

He cleans ROBERTO's *mouth with a napkin.*

ROBERTO. She's going to kill me.

GERARDO. Unless you confess.

ROBERTO. But what can I confess? What can I?

PAULINA. You may be aware, Doctor, that the secret police used some doctors as – consultants in torture sessions . . .

ROBERTO. The Medical Council gradually learned of these situations, and looked into them wherever possible.

GERARDO. She is convinced that you are one of those doctors. So unless you have a way of denying it . . .

ROBERTO. How could I deny it? I'd have to change my voice, prove that this is not my voice. There's no other evidence, nothing that –

GERARDO. She mentioned your skin.

ROBERTO. My skin?

GERARDO. And your smell.

ROBERTO. The fantasies of a diseased mind. She could have latched onto any man coming through that door . . .

GERARDO. Unfortunately, you came through that door.

ROBERTO. Look, Gerardo, I'm a quiet man. Anyone can see that I'm incapable of violence – violence of any sort sickens me. I come to my beach house, I wander on the beach, I watch the waves, I hunt for pebbles, I listen to my music –

GERARDO. Schubert?

ROBERTO. Schubert. Also Vivaldi and Mozart and Telemann. And for some reason yesterday I brought the Schubert with me in the car. And for some even more stupid reason I stopped on the motorway for some lunatic waving his arms like a windmill. Look, it's up to you to get me out of here.

GERARDO. I know.

ROBERTO. Everything hurts, my ankles, my hands, my back. Couldn't you untie me a little, so –

GERARDO. Roberto, I want to be honest with you. There is only one way to save your life . . .

Brief pause.

I think we have to – indulge her.

ROBERTO. Indulge her?

GERARDO. Make her feel that we – that you, are willing to cooperate . . .

ROBERTO. I don't see how I can cooperate, given my rather peculiar position . . .

GERARDO. Indulge her, make her believe that you . . .

ROBERTO. Make her believe that I . . .

GERARDO. She promised me that if you – confessed she would be ready to –

ROBERTO. I haven't got anything to confess!

GERARDO. I think you're going to have to invent something then, because the only way she'll pardon you is if –

ROBERTO (*raises his voice, indignant*). She's got nothing to pardon me for. I did nothing and there's nothing to confess. Do you understand?

Upon hearing ROBERTO's *voice,* PAULINA *gets up from her seat on the terrace and starts to move towards them.*

Instead of proposing dishonourable solutions to me, you should be out there convincing that madwoman of yours to cease this criminal behaviour before she ruins your brilliant career and ends up in gaol or in an asylum. Tell her that. Or can't you impose a little order in your own house?

GERARDO. Roberto, I –

PAULINA *enters from the terrace.*

PAULINA. Spot of trouble, darling?

GERARDO. None.

PAULINA. I thought you looked a little . . . agitated.

Brief pause.

Well, I see you've both finished your soup. No one
can say I'm not a good cook, can they? That I'm not
an ideal housewife? Little cup of coffee, Doctor?
Teensy weensy one? Doctor, I am talking to you.
Didn't your mother ever teach you that . . .

ROBERTO. Leave my mother out of this. I forbid you
to mention my mother.

Brief pause.

PAULINA. I'm sorry, you're absolutely right. Your
mother is not responsible for what you do. I don't
know why men always insist on attacking mothers
instead of –

GERARDO. Paulina, would you please do me the
favour of leaving so we can continue our
conversation?

PAULINA. Okay. I'll leave you boys to fix the world.

She leaves and turns.

Oh, and if he wants to piss, darling, just snap your
fingers and I'll come running.

She returns to the same spot on the terrace, watching.

ROBERTO. She's absolutely insane.

GERARDO. When crazy people have power, you've got
to indulge them. In her case, a confession –

ROBERTO. But what could a confession – ?

GERARDO. I think I understand Paulina's need. It
coincides with a need of the whole country. The need
to put into words what happened to us.

ROBERTO. You believe her, don't you?

GERARDO. If I thought you were guilty, would I be
trying so desperately to save your –

ROBERTO. From the beginning you've been
conspiring with her. She plays the bad guy. You play
the good.

GERARDO. What do you mean by good –

ROBERTO. Playing roles, she's bad, you're good, to see
if you can get me to confess that way. And once
you've got me to confess, not her, she's not going to
do it, you will kill me. It's what any man would do,
any real man, if they'd raped his wife, it's what I
would do if somebody had raped my wife. Cut your
balls off.

Pause. GERARDO *stands up.*

Where are you going?

GERARDO. I'm going to get the gun and blow your
fucking brains out. That's what a real man does,
doesn't he. Real macho men blow people's brains out
and fuck women when they're tied up on cots. Not
like me. I'm a stupid faggot because I defend the son
of a bitch who screwed my wife and destroyed her
entire life. How many times did you screw her? How
many times, you bastard?

ROBERTO. Gerardo, I . . . –

GERARDO. Gerardo, the faggot, is gone. I'm here. Me.
But thinking it over, why should I dirty my hands
with scum like you – when there's somebody who'll
take much more pleasure in your pain and your
death? Why take that one pleasure away from her?
I'll call her right away so she can blow your fucking
brains out herself.

ROBERTO. Don't go. Don't call her.

GERARDO. I'm tired of being in the middle of this.
You reach an understanding with her, you convince
her.

ROBERTO. Gerardo, I'm scared.

Brief pause. GERARDO *turns around, changes his tone.*

GERARDO. So am I.

ROBERTO. Don't let her kill me.

Brief pause.

What are you going to say to her?

GERARDO. The truth. That you won't cooperate.

ROBERTO. I need to know what it is I did, you've got to understand that I don't know what I have to confess. If I were that man, I'd know every – detail, but I don't know anything. If I make a mistake, she'll think I'm – I'll need your help.

GERARDO. You're asking me to deceive my wife?

ROBERTO. I'm asking you to save the life of an innocent man, Escobar. You do believe that I'm innocent, don't you?

GERARDO. You care that much what I believe?

ROBERTO. Of course I do. She isn't the voice of civilisation, you are. She isn't a member of the President's Commission, you are.

GERARDO (*bitter, sad*). No, she isn't . . . Who gives a fuck what she thinks. She's just . . .

He starts to leave.

ROBERTO. Wait. Where are you going? What are you going to say to her?

GERARDO. I'm going to tell her that you need to piss.

Lights go down.

ACT THREE

Scene One

Just before evening. PAULINA *and* GERARDO *are outside, on the terrace facing the sea.* ROBERTO *inside, still tied up.* GERARDO *has the cassette-recorder on his lap.*

PAULINA. I don't understand why.

GERARDO. I have to know.

PAULINA. Why?

Brief pause.

GERARDO. Paulina, I love you. I need to hear it from your lips. It's not fair that after so many years the person to tell me, should be him. It would be – intolerable.

PAULINA. Whereas if I tell you it would be – tolerable.

GERARDO. More tolerable than if he tells me first.

PAULINA. I told you some of it already, Gerardo. Wasn't that enough?

GERARDO. Fifteen years ago you started to tell me and then . . .

PAULINA. Did you expect me to keep on talking to you with that bitch there? That bitch came out of your bedroom half naked asking why you were taking so long, and you expected me to –

GERARDO. She wasn't a bitch.

PAULINA. Did she know where I was? Of course she did. A bitch.

GERARDO. We're not going to start all this again, Paulina.

PAULINA. You're the one who started.

GERARDO. How many times do I have to . . . ? – I'd

spent two months trying to find you. Then she came by, she said she could help. We had a couple of drinks. My God, I'm also human.

PAULINA. While I defended your life, while your name stayed inside me and never left my mouth, – ask him, ask Miranda if I ever so much as whispered your name, while you . . .

GERARDO. You already forgave me, you forgave me, how many times will we have to go over this? We'll die from so much past, we'll suffocate. Let's finish this. Let's close this book once and for all and never speak about it, ever again.

PAULINA. Forgive and forget, eh?

GERARDO. Forgive yes, forget no. But forgive so we can start again. There's so much to live for, my . . .

PAULINA. What did you want me to do, to talk in front of her? To tell you, what they did to me, in front of her, that I should – ? How many times?

GERARDO. How many times what?

PAULINA. How many times did you fuck her?

GERARDO. Paulina . . .

PAULINA. How many?

GERARDO. Baby . . .

PAULINA. How many times did you do it? How many, how many? I tell you, you tell me.

GERARDO (*desperate, shaking her and then taking her in his arms*). Paulina, Paulina. You want to destroy me? Is that what you want?

PAULINA. No.

GERARDO. Well, you're going to. You're going to end up in a world where I don't exist, where I won't be here. Is that what you want?

PAULINA. I want to know how many times you fucked that bitch.

GERARDO. Don't do this to me, Paulina.

PAULINA. That wasn't the first night, was it, Gerardo? You'd seen her before, right? The truth, Gerardo.

GERARDO. Even if it destroys us?

PAULINA. How many times, Gerardo. You tell me, I tell you.

GERARDO. Twice.

PAULINA. That night. What about before that night?

GERARDO (*very low*). Three times.

PAULINA. What?

GERARDO. Three times.

PAULINA. She was that good? You liked her that much? And she liked it too. She must have really enjoyed it if she came back for –

GERARDO. Do you understand what you're doing to me?

PAULINA. Beyond redemption, huh?

GERARDO (*desperate*). What more do you want from me? We survived the dictatorship, we survived, and now we're going to do to each other what those bastards out there weren't able to do to us. You want that?

PAULINA (*quietly*). No.

GERARDO. You want me to leave? Is that what you want? You want me to go out that door and never see you again? God in Heaven, is that what you want?

PAULINA. No.

GERARDO. That's what you're going to get. People can also die from an excessive dose of the truth, you know.

Brief pause.

I'm in your hands like a baby, I have no defences now. You want to treat me like you treat the man who –

PAULINA. No.

GERARDO. You want me to . . . ?

PAULINA (*murmuring*). I want you. You. I want you inside me, alive. I want you making love to me without ghosts in bed and I want you on the Commission defending the truth and I want you in the air I breathe and I want you in my Schubert that I can start listening to again and I want you adopting a child together . . . .

GERARDO. Yes, Paulina, yes, yes.

PAULINA. – and I want to care for you minute by minute like you took care of me after that night –

GERARDO. Never mention that bitch of a night again. If you go on and on about that night, you'll – kill me. Is that what you want?

PAULINA. No.

GERARDO. Are you going to tell me then?

PAULINA. Yes.

GERARDO. Everything?

PAULINA. Everything.

GERARDO. That's the way, that's how we'll get out of this mess, – without hiding a thing from each other, together.

PAULINA. That's the way.

GERARDO. I'm going to switch on the recorder. You don't mind, love, if I switch it on?

PAULINA. Switch it on.

GERARDO *switches it on*.

GERARDO. Just as if you were sitting in front of the Commission.

PAULINA. I don't know how to begin.

GERARDO. Begin with your name.

PAULINA. My maiden name is Paulina Salas. Now I am married to Gerardo Escobar, the lawyer, but at that time –

GERARDO. Date . . .

PAULINA. April 6th, 1975, I was single. I was walking along San Antonio Street –

GERARDO. Be as precise as you can.

PAULINA. – at about two fifteen in the afternoon, and when I reached the corner at Huerfanos street I heard a noise behind me – three men got out of a car, one of them stuck a gun in my back, 'One word and we'll blow your face off, Miss.' He spat the words into my ear – he had garlic on his breath. I was surprised that I should focus on such an insignificant detail, the lunch he had eaten, began to think about how he was digesting that food with all the organs that I had been studying in anatomy. Later on I'd reproach myself, why didn't I call out, I knew that if that happened you're supposed to scream, so people can know who is – call out your name, I'm Paulina Salas, they're taking me, if you don't scream out that first moment you're already defeated, and I submitted too easily, obeyed them right away without even a gesture of defiance. All my life, I've always been much too obedient.

The lights begin to go down.

I met Dr Miranda for the first time three days later when . . . That's when I met Dr Miranda.

The lights go down further and PAULINA*'s voice continues in the darkness, only the cassette-recorder lit by the light of the moon.*

At first, I thought he would save me. He was so soft, so – nice, after what the others had done to me. And then, all of a sudden, I heard the Schubert. There is no way of describing what it means to hear that wonderful music in the darkness, when you haven't eaten for three days, when your body is falling apart, when . . .

In the darkness, we hear ROBERTO*'s voice.*

ROBERTO'S VOICE. I would put on the music because it helped me in my role, the role of good guy, as they call it, I would put on Schubert because it was a way of gaining the prisoners' trust. But I also

knew it was a way of alleviating their suffering.
You've got to believe it was a way of alleviating the
prisoners' suffering. Not only the music, but
everything else I did. That's how they approached
me, at first. The prisoners were dying on them, they
told me, they needed someone to help care for them,
someone they could trust. I've got a brother, who was
a member of the secret services. You can pay the
communists back for what they did to Dad, he told
me one night – my father had a heart attack the day
the peasants took over his land at Las Toltecas. The
stroke paralysed him – he lost his capacity for speech,
would spend hours simply looking at me; his eyes
said, 'Do something'. But that's not why I accepted.
The real real truth, it was for humanitarian reasons.
We're at war, I thought, they want to kill me and my
family, they want to install a totalitarian dictatorship,
but even so, they still have the right to some form of
medical attention. It was slowly, almost without
realising how, that I became involved in more
delicate operations, they let me sit in on sessions
where my role was to determine if the prisoners
could take that much torture, that much electric
current. At first I told myself that it was a way of
saving people's lives, and I did, because many times I
told them – without it being true, simply to help the
person who was being tortured – I ordered them to
stop or the prisoner would die. But afterwards I
began to – bit by bit, the virtue I was feeling turned
into excitement – the mask of virtue fell off it and it,
the excitement, it hid, it hid, it hid from me what I
was doing, the swamp of what – . By the time Paulina
Salas was brought in it was already too late. Too late.

*The lights go up as if the moon were coming out. It is
night-time.* ROBERTO *is in front of the cassette-recorder,
confessing.*

ROBERTO. . . . too late. A kind of – brutalisation took
over my life, I began to really truly like what I was
doing. It became a game. My curiosity was partly
morbid, partly scientific. How much can this woman
take? More than the other one? Does her sex dry up
when you put the current through her? Can she have
an orgasm under those circumstances? She is entirely

in your power, you can carry out all your fantasies, you can do what you want with her.

The moonlight begins to fade and only remains on the cassette-recorder, while ROBERTO's *voice speaks on in the darkness.*

Everything they have forbidden you since ever, whatever your mother ever urgently whispered you were never to do. Come on, Doctor, they would say to me, you're not going to refuse free meat, are you, one of them would sort of taunt me. His name was – let's see – they called him Bud, no, it was Stud – a nickname, because I never found out his real name. They like it, Doctor, Stud would say to me – all these bitches like it and if you put on that sweet little music of yours, they'll get even cosier. He would say this in front of the women, in front of Paulina Salas he would say it, and finally I, finally I – but not one ever died on me, not one of the women, not one of the men.

The lights go up and it is now dawning. ROBERTO, *untied, writes on a sheet of paper his own words from the cassette-recorder. In front of him, many sheets of handwritten pages.* PAULINA *and* GERARDO *watch him.*

ROBERTO'S VOICE (*from the recorder*). To the best of my memory, I took part in the – interrogation of 94 prisoners, including Paulina Salas. It is all I can say. I ask forgiveness.

GERARDO *switches off the cassette-recorder while* ROBERTO *writes.*

ROBERTO. – forgiveness.

GERARDO *switches the cassette-recorder back on.*

ROBERTO'S VOICE. And I hope that this confession proves that I feel real repentance and that just as the country is reaching reconciliation and peace . . .

GERARDO *switches off the cassette-recorder.*

GERARDO. Did you write that? Just as the country is reaching reconciliation and peace?

He switches it on again.

ROBERTO'S VOICE. – so too should I be allowed to live the rest of my days with my terrible secret. There can be no worse punishment than that which is imposed upon me by the voice of my conscience.

ROBERTO (*while he writes*) – punishment . . . my conscience.

GERARDO *switches off the cassette-recorder. A moment's silence.*

And now what? You want me to sign?

PAULINA. First write there that this is all done of your own free will, without any sort of pressure whatsoever.

ROBERTO. That's not true.

PAULINA. You want pressure, Doctor?

ROBERTO *writes down a couple of phrases, shows them to* GERARDO, *who moves his head affirmatively.*

PAULINA. Now you can sign.

ROBERTO *signs.* PAULINA *looks at the signature, collects the paper, takes the cassette out of the recorder.*

Have you noticed how splendid the dawns are here when the sea is stormy?

GERARDO. Paulina.

PAULINA. Do you know how I feel right now, Gerardo? I feel free. Not like the sun, because the sun, poor thing, has to come out every day in the same place, almost at the same time, always the same route across the sky. I feel like that seagull, like that wave, like the air. Everything is really still ahead of me, it's not a lie when we say that all of our life is still ahead of us.

GERARDO. Paulina. It's over. It is over. Don't you think it's about time we . . .

PAULINA. Right. We had an agreement. I'm glad to see that you're still a man of principles. I thought I'd have to convince you now, now that you know he really is guilty, I thought I'd have to convince you not to kill him.

GERARDO. I would not stain my soul with someone like him.

PAULINA (*throws him the keys to the car*). He's free. You just have to go and get his car.

GERARDO *begins to untie* ROBERTO'*s ankles.*

I don't think you understood me, Gerardo. When I said you, I didn't mean both of you.

GERARDO. What are you talking about?

PAULINA. I'm not letting him go alone with you.

GERARDO. Paulina, we agreed that . . . ?

PAULINA. Didn't you hear what this man just confessed? He's violent and dangerous.

GERARDO. He's a poor defeated bastard. When somebody confesses like that, degrades himself in that way – he can't hurt you anymore, Paulina.

PAULINA. You're the one he can hurt.

ROBERTO. How could I possibly harm the man who –

PAULINA. You can overpower him, you can run him over – come back here and take these papers and the cassette and – I know you, Doctor. There is no way I am going to leave him alone with you, Gerardo.

GERARDO. All right, all right, I'll go get the car.

He stands up and goes towards the door.

PAULINA. Oh, Gerardo. Don't forget to give his jack back.

GERARDO (*trying to smile*). And don't you forget to return his Schubert cassette. You have your own.

Brief pause.

Take care of yourself.

He exits. PAULINA *goes to the window, watches him leave.*

ROBERTO. If you wouldn't mind, I would like to go to the bathroom. I suppose there is no reason why you should continue to accompany me?

PAULINA. Don't move, Doctor. There's still a little matter pending. (*Brief pause.*) It's going to be an incredibly beautiful day. You know the only thing that's missing now, Doctor, the one thing I need to make this day really truly perfect? (*Brief pause.*) To kill you. So I can listen to my Schubert without thinking that you'll also be listening to it, soiling my day and my seagull and my Schubert and my country and my husband. That's what I need . . .

ROBERTO. Madame, your husband left here trusting that you – . . . You gave your word . . .

PAULINA. But when I gave my word – I still had a doubt – a teensy weensy doubt – that you really were that man. Because Gerardo was right, in his way. Proof, hard proof – well, I could have been mistaken. But I knew that if you confessed, – and when I heard you, my last doubts vanished and now I want you dead. Now that I know, now, that you are that man, I could not live in peace with myself and let you live.

She points the gun at him.

You have a minute to pray and really repent, Doctor.

Roberto slowly stands.

ROBERTO. Don't do it. I'm innocent.

PAULINA. You've confessed, Doctor.

ROBERTO. It's false, ma'am.

PAULINA. What do you mean?

ROBERTO. I made it up. We made it up.

PAULINA. It seems very true to me, Doctor, painfully familiar as far as I'm concerned . . .

ROBERTO. Your husband told me what to write, I invented some of it, some of it was invented by me, but most of it was what he got from you, from what he knew had happened to you, ma'am, so you'd let me go, he convinced me that it was the only way that you wouldn't kill me and I had to – you must know how, under pressure, we say anything, but I'm innocent, ma'am, God in Heaven knows that –

PAULINA. Stud, Doctor.

ROBERTO. What?

PAULINA. Several times in your confession you mention Stud. He must have been a large man, muscular, he bit his fingernails, right, he bit his goddam fingernails. Stud.

ROBERTO. The name was given to me by your husband. Everything I said comes from what your husband helped me to invent. Ask him when he comes back.

PAULINA. I don't need to ask him. I knew that he'd do that, I knew he'd use my words for your confession. That's the sort of person he is. He always thinks that he's more intelligent than everybody else, he always thinks that he's got to save somebody. But I don't blame him, Doctor. He loves me. We deceived each other for our own good, because we love each other. But I'm the one who came out on top in this game. I gave him the wrong name, Doctor, to see if you would correct it. And you did. You corrected the name Bud and you substituted the name Stud and if you were innocent – .

ROBERTO. It's a mere coincidence, it's natural that I should think it was Stud rather than Bud, because it would be a natural for that sort of person to –

PAULINA. It's not the only correction that you made, Doctor. There were other . . . lies.

ROBERTO. What lies, what lies?

PAULINA. Tiny lies, little variations that I inserted in my story to Gerardo, and often – not always, but often enough – as in the case of Stud, you corrected them. It turned out just as I planned. You were so scared that if you didn't get it right . . . But I'm not going to kill you because you're guilty, Doctor, but because you haven't repented at all. I can only forgive someone who really repents, who stands up amongst those he has wronged and says, I did this, I did it, and I'll never do it again.

ROBERTO. What more do you want? You've got more than all the victims in this country will ever get. A man who's confessed, at your feet, humiliated,

He gets down on his knees.

begging for his life. What more do you want?

PAULINA. The truth, Doctor. The truth and I'll let you go. Then you'll be free as Cain after he killed his brother. Nobody dared touch Cain after he repented – that's why God marked him. The truth. Confess and I'll let you go. You have ten seconds. One, two, three, four, five, six, seven, eight. Time is running out, Doctor. Confess!

ROBERTO *stands up.*

ROBERTO. No. I won't. Because even if I confess, you'll never be satisfied. You're going to kill me anyway. So go ahead and kill me. I'm not going to let any sick woman treat me like this. If you want to kill me, do it. But you're killing an innocent man.

PAULINA. Nine.

ROBERTO. So we go on and on with violence, always more violence. Yesterday they did terrible things to you and now you do terrible things to me and tomorrow the same cycle will begin all over again. Isn't it time we stopped?

PAULINA. Why is it always people like me who have to sacrifice, who have to concede when concessions are needed, biting my tongue, why? Well, not this time. If only to do justice in one case, just one. What do we lose? What do we lose by killing one of you? What do we lose?

They freeze in their position as the lights begin to go down slowly. We begin to hear music from the last movement of Mozart's Dissonant Quartet. PAULINA and ROBERTO are covered from view by a giant mirror which descends, forcing the audience to look at themselves. For a few minutes, the Mozart quartet is heard, while the spectators watch themselves in the mirror.

Scene Two

A concert hall. An evening some months later. GERARDO *and* PAULINA *appear, elegantly dressed. They sit down facing the mirror, their backs to the spectators, perhaps in two chairs or in two of the seats in the audience itself. Under the music we can hear typical sounds of an audience during a concert: throats clearing, an occasional cough, the ruffling of programme notes, even some heavy breathing. When the music ends,* GERARDO *begins to applaud and we can hear the applause growing from what is an invisible public.*
PAULINA *does not applaud. The applause begins to die down and then we hear the habitual sounds that come from a concert hall when the first part of a programme is over: more throat clearing, murmurs, bodies shuffling toward the foyer. They both begin to go out, greeting people, stopping to chat for an instant. They slowly distance themselves from their seats and advance along an imaginary foyer which is apparently full of spectators. We hear mutterings, etc.* GERARDO *begins to talk to members of the audience, as if they were at the concert. His words can be heard above the murmurs of the public.*

GERARDO (*intimately, talking to diverse spectators*). Why, thank you, thank you so much. Yes, we feel that the Final Report of the Commission is quite extraordinary . . . Yes, I do think that the whole country is going to benefit from it, yes, reconciliation is really served by –

PAULINA *slowly leaves him, going to one side where a small bar has been installed.* GERARDO *continues speaking with his audience until she returns.*

People are acting with enormous generosity, without the hint of seeking a personal vendetta. Ah, that experience, the one I mentioned in the interview? You'd have been moved too if you'd seen her. The woman was timid. She began to speak standing up. 'Please sit down,' the President of the Commission said and stood up to hold her chair for her. She sat down and began to sob. Then she looked at us and said: 'This is the first time, sir,' she said to us – her husband had disappeared fourteen years ago, and she had spent thousands of hours, thousands of hours petitioning, thousands of hours waiting – 'This is the first time,' she said to us,' in all these years, sir, that somebody asks me to sit down.'

Meanwhile, PAULINA *has bought some candy — and as she pays,* ROBERTO *enters, under a light which has a faint phantasmagoric moonlight quality. He could be real or he could be an illusion in* PAULINA's *head.* PAULINA *does not see him yet. She returns to* GERARDO's *side who, by this time, should be finishing his monologue.*
ROBERTO *stays behind, watching* PAULINA *and* GERARDO *from a distance.*

The officials who should have been helping her had spent all these years calling her a madwoman and a liar, and all of a sudden, there she is, able to recount her pain to a Commission officially named by the President of the Republic. The dignity she had always privately possessed was now conferred upon her publicly, her words were really worth something. Now that's priceless. She and her family have been vindicated, publicly reintegrated into the community.

A bell goes off to indicate that the concert is about to recommence.

As for the murderers, even if we do not know or cannot reveal their names — Ah, Paulinetta, just in time. This is about to start. You certainly took your time. Well, I'll see you later, old man. Yes, I agree. This country *has* been sick for far too long. I can only hope that our work will help in the slow, patient process of healing.
All right, old man, later for sure. Now I've finally got some free time. Maybe we could have a couple of drinks at home. Pau mixes a cocktail that'll put your hair on end.

GERARDO *and* PAULINA *sit in their seats.*
ROBERTO *goes to another seat, always looking at* PAULINA. *Applause is heard when the imaginary musicians come on. The instruments are tested and tuned. Then 'Death and the Maiden' begins.* GERARDO *looks at* PAULINA *who looks forward. He takes her hand and then also begins to look forward. After a few instants, she turns slowly and looks at* ROBERTO. *Their eyes interlock for a moment. Then she turns her head and faces the stage and*

the mirror. The lights go down while the music plays and plays and plays.

Afterword

Eight or nine years ago, when General Augusto Pinochet was still the dictator of Chile and I was still in exile, I began tentatively exploring in my mind a dramatic situation that was someday to become the core of *Death and the Maiden*. A man whose car breaks down on the motorway is given a lift home by a friendly stranger. The man's wife, believing she recognises in the stranger the voice of the torturer who raped her some years before, kidnaps him and decides to put him on trial. On several occasions I sat down to scribble what I then imagined would be a novel. A few hours and a couple of unsatisfactory pages later, I would give up in frustration. Something essential was missing. I could not figure out, for instance, who the woman's husband was, how he would react to her violence, if he would believe her. Nor were the historical circumstances under which the story developed clear to me, the symbolic and secret connections to the larger life of the country itself, the world beyond the narrow claustrophobic boundaries of that woman's home. The use of a forceps may be necessary to ensure the birth of a child that needs help getting out of the womb, but I had by then blessedly learned that when characters do not want to be born forceps may hurt them permanently and irreparably twist their lives. My trio would, unfortunately, have to wait.

They were forced to wait a long time. It was not until Chile returned to democracy in 1990 and I myself therefore returned to resettle there with my family after seventeen years of exile, that I finally understood how the story had to be told.

My country was at the time (and still is now as I write this) living an uneasy transition to democracy, with Pinochet no longer the President but still in command of the Armed Forces, still able to threaten another coup if people became unruly or, more specifically, if attempts were made to punish the human rights' violations of the outgoing regime. And in order to avoid chaos and constant confrontation, the new government had to find a way of not alienating Pinochet supporters who continued occupying significant areas of power in the Judiciary, the Senate,

the Town Councils – and particularly the economy. In
the area of human rights, our democratically elected
President, Patricio Aylwin, responded to this quandary
by naming a Commission – called the Rettig
Commission after the eighty-year-old lawyer who
headed it – that would investigate the crimes of the
dictatorship that had ended in death or its
presumption, but which would neither name the
perpetrators nor judge them. This was an important
step towards healing a sick country: the truth of the
terror unleashed upon us that we had always known in
a private and fragmented fashion would finally receive
public recognition, established forever as official
history, recreating a community fractured by divisions
and hatred that we wished to leave behind. On the
other hand, justice would not be done and the
traumatic experience of hundreds of thousands of
other victims, those who had survived, would not even
be addressed. Aylwin was steering a prudent but valiant
course between those who wanted past terror totally
buried and those who wanted it totally revealed.

As I watched with fascination how the Commission
carried out its difficult task, it slowly dawned on me
that here might be the key to the unresolved story that
had been buzzing inside my head for so many years:
that kidnapping and trial would occur, not in a nation
under the boot of a dictator, but in one that was in
transition to democracy, where so many Chileans were
grappling with the hidden traumas of what had been
done to them while other Chileans wondered if their
crimes would now be revealed. It also became clear that
the way to make the husband of the tortured woman
have a tremendous stake in the outcome of that
kidnapping was to make him a member of a
Commission similar to the one headed by Rettig. And it
did not take me long to conclude that, rather than a
novel, what needed to be written was a play.

It was a risky idea. I knew from experience that
distance is often the best ally of an author and that
when we deal with events that are being enacted and
multiplied in immediate history, a danger always exists
of succumbing to a 'documentary' or overly realistic
approach, losing universality and creative freedom,
trying to adjust the characters to the events unfolding

around us rather than letting them emerge on their own and, letting them surprise and disturb us. I also knew that I would be savagely criticised by some in my own country for 'rocking the boat' by reminding everyone about the long-term effects of terror and violence on people precisely at a time when we were being asked to be notably cautious.

I felt, however, that, if as a citizen I had to be responsible and reasonable, as an artist I had to answer the wild mating call of my characters and break the silence which was weighing upon so many of my self-censored compatriots, fearful of creating 'trouble' for the new democracy. It was then and is now more than ever my belief that a fragile democracy is strengthened by expressing for all to see the deep dramas and sorrows and hopes that underlie its existence and that it is not by hiding the damage we have inflicted on ourselves that we will avoid its repetition.

As I began to write I found the characters trying to figure out the questions that so many Chileans were asking themselves privately but that hardly anyone seemed interested in posing in public. How can those who tortured and those who were tortured co-exist in the same land? How to heal a country that has been traumatised by repression if the fear to speak out is still omnipresent everywhere? And how do you reach the truth if lying has become a habit? How do we keep the past alive without becoming its prisoner? How do we forget it without risking its repetition in the future? Is it legitimate to sacrifice the truth to ensure peace? And what are the consequences of suppressing that past and the truth it is whispering or howling to us? Are people free to search for justice and equality if the threat of a military intervention haunts them? And given these circumstances, can violence be avoided? And how guilty are we all of what happened to those who suffered most? And perhaps the greatest dilemma of them all: how to confront these issues without destroying the national consensus which creates democratic stability?

Three weeks later, *Death and the Maiden* was ready.

If the play revealed many of the hidden conflicts that were just under the surface of the nation, and therefore posed a clear threat to people's psychological security, it also could be an instrument through which they explored their identity and the contradictory options available to us in the years to come.

A multitude of messages of the contemporary imagination, specifically those that are channelled through the mass entertainment media, assure us, over and over, that there is an easy, even facile, comforting, answer to most of our problems. Such an aesthetic strategy seems to me not only to falsify and disdain human experience but in the case of Chile or of any country that is coming out of a period of enormous conflict and pain, it turns out to be counterproductive for the community, freezes its maturity and growth. I felt that *Death and the Maiden* touched upon a desire I had nursed for a long time: to write a contemporary tragedy in an almost Aristotelian sense, a work of art that might help a collective to purge itself, through pity and terror, in other words to force the spectators to confront those predicaments which, if not brought into the light of day, could lead to their ruin.

Which is a way of stating that this piece of fiction, as so much of what I had written previously in my novels, stories, poems and other plays, was not merely Chilean in scope but addressed problems that could be found all over the world, all over the twentieth century, all over the face of humanity through the ages. It was not only about a country that is afraid and simultaneously needful of understanding its fear and its scars, not only about the long-term effects of torture and violence on human beings and the beautiful body of their land, but about other themes that have always obsessed me: what happens when women take power, how can you tell the truth if the mask you have adopted ends up being identical to your face, how does memory beguile and save and guide us, how can we keep our innocence once we have tasted evil, how to forgive those who have hurt us irreparably, how to find a language that is political but not pamphletary, how to tell stories that are both popular and ambiguous, stories that can be understood by large audiences and yet contain stylistic experimentation, that are mythical and also about immediate human beings?

Death and the Maiden appears in English at a moment when humanity is undergoing extraordinary changes,

when there is great hope for the future and great
confusion about what that future might bring. In the
current debate, little is being heard from that
submerged zone of our species, those who live far from
the centres of power but are often near to the quick
centre of suffering where ethical choices determine the
immediate shape of things to come and things to be
postponed. In times such as these, when the more
miserable and distant lands seem to disappear from the
horizon, it may help us a bit, perhaps a teensy weensy
bit, I would hope, to think of the Paulinas, the
Gerardos, the Robertos, of the world – to figure out for
ourselves which of these three we most resemble, how
much of our secluded lives are expressed in each of
these characters and in all of them. Until finally, I
would also hope, we would realise that what we feel
when we watch and whisper and ache with these
faraway people from faraway Chile could well be that
strange trembling state of humanity we call recognition,
a bridge across our divided globe.

Ariel Dorfman
11 September 1991.

This special programme edition of *Death and the Maiden*
first published in 1992 by Nick Hern Books, a Random
Century Company, 20 Vauxhall Bridge Road, London
SW1V 2SA in association with the Royal Court Theatre,
Sloane Square, London SW1W 8AS. Originally
published as a paperback original in 1991 by Nick Hern
Books.

Death and the Maiden translated from the Spanish
original *La Muerte y la Doncella* by Ariel Dorfman.
Copyright © 1990 by Ariel Dorfman

Set in Baskerville by 𝐀 Tek Art Ltd,
Addiscombe, Croydon, Surrey
Printed in Great Britain by Cox & Wyman Ltd,
Reading, Berkshire

ISBN: 0-71264-451-2

Front cover: detail from Edvard Munch's *Das Mädchen
und der Tod*, 1984, copyright Munch Museum, Oslo.
Reproduced with permission.